HELLO
MY LOVES

For Norm &
Heidi
With Thanks For
All your Love &
Support !

Also by
Wayne (Ram Tzu) Liquorman:

NO WAY for the Spiritually "Advanced"

Acceptance of What IS...a book about Nothing

Never Mind

Enlightenment is Not What You Think

HELLO
MY LOVES

10 years of writings to seekers of Truth

Wayne Liquorman

EDITED BY PAUL RATHJE

Advaita Press

For Jaki
Who brightened these years

PREFACE

These letters were written between 2004 and 2013 for inclusion in newsletters Wayne sent to spiritual seekers around the world. They describe his experience of teaching Advaita, which he now also calls *The Living Teaching*. They document his travels, his relationship with Ramesh Balsekar, his reactions to current events, and answers to questions from spiritual seekers. Though they weren't originally intended for a book, they are such an affecting journal of births and deaths, of Wayne's family and of the larger family of seekers, and of the development of this *Teaching*. They cover the global and the personal in a familiar arc that always points back to the same place. Whether read through at a single sitting, or one a day, or dipped into at random, they make interesting reading.

If you've been to an Advaita Talk at Wayne's house you may recognize the beautiful Koi fish — mysterious, friendly, brilliant and inquisitive.

Paul Rathje

Happy New Year to you!

As I prepare to go to visit my beloved Ramesh I am struck with the wonder that is this Life. The sheer vastness and variety of experience in this manifest world is awesome in its magnitude. That we can Love so deeply, feel so richly and hurt so excruciatingly fills me with gratitude for this gift of life.

My New Years wish for all of us is that in the coming year we get everything we need and not everything we deserve.

With much love,

Wayne

Hello my loves,

As always it was an incredible joy to be with my beloved Ramesh in Bombay last month. He is in fine form, healthy and robust and as razor sharp and Loving as ever. Even though it was the height of the "seeker season" (January is when Bombay is at its most pleasant weatherwise) there were rarely more than 40 people at the Talks Ramesh gives daily at his flat. It always surprises me that there aren't 10,000 people camped out at Ramesh's door but Ramesh has often reminded us that this Teaching has never been one for the masses of people. Those of us that have been led to him and to his Advaita consider ourselves fortunate indeed.

Ramesh's Teaching continues to evolve and expand. Today Ramesh's emphasis is on "ease and comfort in day to day living" and a new book with that slant is due to be published shortly.

Some photos from the trip can be found... on the advaita. org website. ENJOY!!

With much love,

Wayne

Hello my loves,

Everyone is talking about THE WAR because the news is talking about THE WAR. The Teaching of Advaita has no position on such matters other than to point to the fact that war exists. Acceptance of this fact leads to a peace that exists at the center of the storm. This peace may exist along with actions that represent opposition to whatever is going on. So it is quite possible to Accept and at the same time march in a peace demonstration or commit a violent act. The Acceptance this Teaching points to underlies action and non-action but advocates neither.

I really enjoyed our trip to Sedona last week. The group there was particularly sweet...interested, loving and alive. And we even got a bit of snow to dust the magnificent red rocks. Some photos from the trip can be found under EVENT PHOTOS on the advaita.org website. ENJOY!!

With much love,

Wayne

Hello my loves,

Yesterday I received a copy of Ramesh's new book, "Peace and Harmony in Daily Living" and I was very impressed with both the content and the layout and design. It is a book that will particularly appeal to someone new to Advaita in that, as the title suggests, it approaches the Teaching from the standpoint of daily living. For the reader more familiar with Ramesh and his Teaching... it is simply a joy, vintage Ramesh presented with the deft touch of his latest editor, Susan Waterman.

It was a pleasure to spend some time with the folks in Boulder last weekend and this weekend I will venture up to Ross in the San Francisco Bay Area where the Talks are always lively and the company eclectic to say the least.

Some photos from the Boulder Talks can be found under EVENT PHOTOS on the advaita.org website. ENJOY!!

With much love,

Wayne

Hello my loves,

I am recently returned home from Europe and I am again struck with what an incredible blessing this Teaching is and how tenacious. It reminds me sometimes of the plant that grows up through a crack in the sidewalk... unexpected and rare and strong. On this trip I met Paolo, who came to the Talks in Rome from his home in Sicily. Somehow a translated copy of "Consciousness Speaks" had found its way into his hands and had affected him deeply. He talked about how the Teaching had changed his life, bringing a sense of Knowingness where before there had only been questions and confusion. As I listened to him and watched the tears of gratitude well up in his eyes I felt renewed.

This Teaching, appreciated by so few, misunderstood by so many, has the power to transform lives in ways unimaginable. It goes where it needs to go, takes root in seemingly the most unlikely of places and just at the moment when we take it for granted it always surprises us.

It is indeed Grace to be the instrument through which this magnificent Teaching happens.

With much love,
Wayne

Hello my loves,

This is the month of Guru Pournima, a time when the Guru (both as the Source and as the teacher) is honored and celebrated. This year the Guru's Full Moon falls on July 13. In Mumbai, at Ramesh's flat, there will be refreshments served (Ramesh's wife Sharda will provide her famous iced coffee and some lovely sweets). For those of us not fortunate enough to physically make it to India for the occasion we might content ourselves with Ramesh's latest book entitled (aptly enough)... "Guru Pournima" in which Ramesh and some of us who love him have written about this most joyous and profound of all human relationships.

So consider yourself warned! If you are unable to come to the Talk, please join us via the live webcast. Like the Teaching itself, it is free for the taking.

I am very grateful to those who have, through their generosity, made it possible for me to live and Teach. Many of you have offered your love and support either directly or through your membership in the Advaita Fellowship. I want you to know that I have noticed and that I am most appreciative. It matters not if we have spoken or seen each other recently. This relationship makes no demands and has no set form. There are no requirements other than an open heart...and even that is seen as subject to change. So, wherever you find yourself on this Guru Pournima, whatever your current thoughts, whoever you find yourself attracted to....know that you are well and truly Loved.

Wayne

Hello my loves,

I have been at home without traveling for 7 weeks now. This is by far the longest at home period of the year and it has been a pleasure to not have had to fold this big body into a tiny airplane seat. But now it is time to venture forth again and visit some of you in Northern California and Arizona. That is the sweet side to this teaching business.... the wonderful people who have appeared in my life. I consider myself infinitely blessed to encounter so much Love...it seems to appear wherever I travel and when I am at home it just walks in through the front door and sits down. Amazing!

When Jaki and I were in Bombay visiting Ramesh in January we had a chance to preview the work of a very talented film maker named Mutribo, who was working on a series of films about Ramesh. These are now finished and are absolutely magnificent!

One is a set of seven DVD's, each containing an interview with Ramesh. Taken together they are the most comprehensive overview of Ramesh's Teaching currently available. The other is a two DVD set from Ramesh's 2002 Kovalam, India retreat/seminar. The editing and cinematography are superb on all the disks. More information about them can be found below. I can recommend them without reservation. Enjoy!

To those of you who joined us both live and via the web on Guru Purnima and to those who remembered us with gifts and good wishes..... Thank You.

With much love,

Wayne

Hello my loves,

Sometimes I am amazed at the effects of this Teaching. Last month I was visited by a radiologist from Santa Fe, New Mexico who specializes in breast cancer diagnosis. Many times each week he must tell women that they are going to lose their breast or perhaps to die. He described how the Teaching had transformed his approach to his work. Whereas before, he was looking only to get enough money to retire, after the Teaching had "infected" him he found that he approached his work with openness and joy. He described how grateful he was to be able to witness the incredible strength and dignity some of these women exhibited and to participate in their lives.

His story and his display of quiet gratitude moved me deeply. My wish for you all is that you be so blessed.

With much love,

Wayne

Hello my loves,

We are back from Maui where we enjoyed yet another glorious week of heartfelt connection with a wonderful group amidst the incredible natural beauty of that magnificent island.

One afternoon we were driving down a narrow country road through the lush green rainforest. We had just swum in a secluded waterfall pool. We were on our way back from a bit of jagged coastline where we had sat for hours watching the huge waves crash on the black lava rocks sending spires of spray into the unimaginably blue sky.

Through a break in the colorful vegetation we caught a glimpse into the front yard of one of the houses. Amidst the rusted hulks of abandoned cars and appliances was a raised cage containing two woeful, half starved dogs. Other cages contained fighting cocks. Vicious dogs stood chained to stakes in the ground. The whole scene was malevolent and unwholesome. It felt as if a cloud moved in front of the joy that had been shining on us. We drove on.

I was struck with how perfectly this captured the yin and yang of life. Ugliness and beauty are neighbors. Joy and sorrow flow into each other. The Acceptance this teaching points to is that both are essential aspects of life. The same creative energy in the universe is responsible for both. Just as it is the same energy that fuels one person to act cruelly, fuels another to act to stop the cruelty and fuels yet another to write about it. True humility is in realizing that each of us has been created with a role to play and that none of us were consulted beforehand about what that role was to be.

With much love,

Wayne

P.S. I am looking forward to seeing some of you this coming weekend in New York City.

Hello my loves,

In the US we have just finished our Thanksgiving holiday. It is as the name suggest a time for gratitude...an occasion to count ones blessings.

It is a peculiar yet nearly universal quality amongst humans that pain and hardship weigh more than equivalent amounts of pleasure and good fortune. Happiness seems fleeting while misery seems to endure. Like so much in life, these are appearances and appearances can be deceptive.

The essence of this advaitic teaching is to question....to inquire... to seek the Truth behind the appearance. Perhaps if you look closely you will witness the miracles that abound all around you. And if you look very very closely and are very very lucky you may glimpse the Miracle that you truly ARE.

An early holiday gift reached me yesterday in the form of a new book about my beloved guru, Ramesh. It is a biography of his life entitled "THE HAPPENING OF A GURU" and it is truly a thing of beauty. It contains numerous photos of him and his family, as well as photos of his guru, Nisargadatta Maharaj. The accompanying text gives a real sense of Ramesh as a man and a wonderful piece by Ramesh entitled, How Do I Live My Life?, gives the reader an incredible insight into the daily life of this beloved Sage.

Happy holidays

With much love,

Wayne

Hello my loves,

This New Year opens before me like a garden gate and invites me to peer in for a glimpse of what is inside. Filled with plans and imaginings the year ahead beckons. So many invitations from wonderful people all over the world to come and spend some time and talk about this Advaita and to sit quietly in the Silence of What Is... impossible to accept them all but how amazing to be the vessel for such an outpouring of Love and generosity.

Being grounded in the moment is sometimes misunderstood to mean never thinking about the future... but this is, of course, ridiculous. The ability to plan and to consider future outcomes is essential to a rich human life. The sage is capable of making plans but he does not LIVE in the projected results of his plans. Therefore there is no projected fear of what will become of ME if a particular result occurs and in the absence of the projected fear the planning is practical and immediate. Thus it is possible for the sage to both live in the moment and plan for the future.

I am busy now, working on a new book and preparing to visit Ramesh in a few weeks. I feel so blessed to be able to spend the time with him. Visiting one's guru is about the only thing I can think of that beats sex and chocolate.

For those of you I will be seeing in the next few weeks, either here in Hermosa Beach or in Amsterdam, Bombay or London, I will be able to wish you a happy and contented New Year in person. For the rest of you who are reading this, please know that I am delighted to be connected with you through whatever means and I hope that the year 2004 brings you the Peace that surpasses all understanding.

With much love,

Wayne

Hello my loves,

I have recently returned from India where I had the great joy of spending 10 days with my beloved Ramesh. I am very very pleased to report that he is in excellent health and spirits and his Teaching is as potent as ever. To sit in that little room in Bombay and watch Ramesh work his magic is one of life's greatest pleasures. I am often amazed how he meets each person at the point of their current understanding and then guides them deeper, ever deeper. He is truly a Master and his teaching moves with the grace and precision of a great dancer or athlete. His emphasis on peace and harmony in daily living continues to grow stronger. It is as if he is crafting his legacy to the world. Those of us fortunate enough to have spent time with this extraordinary man are very blessed indeed.

I am very pleased that there was sufficient interest to make possible another week-long retreat in Maui at the end of next month. Maui remains one of my favorite places on the planet and the group that gathers for the retreat is always incredibly special. I am always awed at the quality of Silence that emerges after just a few days of being together in that magical place.

It is also wonderful to be home. To sink back into the routine of the house. To meet the loves who visit here for the Talks. To watch the koi swimming in the pond, their scales flashing in the sunlight. To hear the wind rustle the bamboo. To greet the hummingbirds that come to the feeder next to the window. I love the rhythms of this life. It is very good to be alive.

With much love,

Wayne

Hello my loves,

What interests me most is what are often referred to as The Simple Pleasures of Life. It is funny how the word mundane, which means "of this world," has come to suggest something that is boring or trivial, when to my mind the everyday is truly miraculous.

Our culture has speeded up to the point where there is a sense of urgency about everything. There is so much to see and know and do... jets, cell phones, computers, TV's all shrink and speed. But the more we know, the more there is to know. The more we do, the more there is to do. The images flash by so fast that they have to be assaultive to be noticed. What happens is that the senses become overloaded and numb.

Please know that I am not decrying the current state of affairs or calling for a return to pastoral living... rather I am pointing to what is happening. Sometimes, when there is grace, the seeing of what is happening is the conduit for change.

Stop for a moment. Look around. Take a deep breath. Here IT is. God in movement is right in front of your eyes. What a great laugh. The miraculous just sitting there, waiting to be known.

With much love,

Wayne

Hello my loves,

Compassion is a quality that is much valued and discussed in spiritual circles. We need to look at what is generally meant by this term - compassion. The superficial meaning is kindness; a caring, heart-centered interaction, in which the recipient leaves feeling good.

Compassion is actually deeper than that. I have seen what I would consider to be compassion from a sage, specifically Ramesh, which from the standpoint of the recipient was harsh. Ramesh isn't a harsh character, but sometimes the stripping away of a false belief, while compassionate, is not a gentle or sweet action.

As we get older, often we become encrusted with those beliefs that were once used to create a sense of personal security. Of course, it never worked for very long. There is no security in life. The essence of life being change, there's always that underlying tickle of uncertainty, of not being secure. The usual solution to this is to try and patch up the structure by applying new and stronger beliefs.

The sage will sometimes raze the whole structure. Often the demolition of these encrusted false beliefs is a painful process; it leaves a person feeling uncomfortable, discontent, and uncertain. It is, to quote Hafiz, "to take away those toys that bring you no joy."

It's like this - If you see a two-year-old with a sharp knife, and you take it away from him he's going to scream. As far as he's concerned, you've done him a great harm. "That was MY toy. I was having fun with that." Since he was about to chop his leg off and you prevented that from happening, I would say was a compassionate act. But the child doesn't see it as a compassionate act. Similarly, the action of the sage is sometimes not seen as compassionate.

If I had to define compassion, I would say that the compassion of the sage is rooted in total acceptance. In such total acceptance you are accepted completely as you are in the moment, without qualification.

This acceptance is, in fact, an underlying quality to every action by the sage. The action may be to take away the toys, to push the disciple into areas where the disciple isn't comfortable, to ask difficult questions and not let up. So the disciple goes away unhappy. "How can this be compassion? I'm unhappy. He wasn't kind and gentle with me. I feel worse now then I did when I walked in and met him."

It is compassionate for one reason: there is no personal agenda on the part of the sage. Every single act is compassionate because there is no "me" desiring something for itself. This is truly the blessing of the sage.

With much love,

Wayne

Hello my loves,

Since I often start my Talks with the admonition that what I am about to say is not the Truth, people frequently follow that up with the question: So why do you teach?

In short I do not teach. The teaching is expressed without any personal agenda. The expression may come forth as a result of a question from someone, or it may come forth as a burst of creative energy, as in the case of spontaneous poetry or these lines you are reading now. What is absent is the slightest shred of belief that what is being said or being written or being thought is the Truth. Any expression is understood at the most fundamental level to be a pointer, a relative teaching tool. That's why the sage is said to have a natural humility, because there is the total absence of the conviction that what is being expressed is the Truth. The humility comes from the deepest possible conviction that what is being expressed is relative.

So, I personally have no trouble with anyone else's teaching. If one teacher says that you exist and another one says you don't exist, and this one says that you're God incarnate and this other one says that you're nothing, I don't care. They are all understood to be relative teaching tools. There is never a question of the hammer being Truer than the screwdriver. What I find objectionable (in an aesthetic sense) is when someone says, "What I am saying is the truth and what the other teaching is saying is bullshit." Such an assertion lacks the essential clarity of understanding that it's ALL bullshit, and that a given teacher's teaching is simply a matter of enculturation and personal programing that determine how their teaching is expressed.

As you navigate the shifting reefs and shoals of the spiritual sea it may be useful to remember that that which is the most solid is also the most likely to sink you.

With love,

Wayne

Hello my loves,

There is a prevalent notion that there can be Awakening or Realization that comes and goes and finally stabilizes after some time. I do not believe that there is such a thing as partial realization. I recognize there is seeking. I recognize there is intellectual understanding and there is spiritual experience, both of which are progressive and cumulative. And I recognize there is the final understanding, which is sudden, irrevocable, and after which there can be no further process, in the same way that you cannot be more dead. You can only be dead; you can't be dead plus. Once dead, there is no question of stabilizing into your deadness. And realization, or the final understanding, is exactly like that.

In my definition of this final understanding, gradual or evolutionary enlightenment is not possible. What that refers to is this unveiling process of seeking in which you have spiritual insights. In that stage, there are often very real spiritual experiences in which you know the oneness of things. Such experiences ebb, and then they often come back again. That's what I call the process of spiritual seeking. This process has increasingly been redefined as enlightenment or awakening. In fact, much of the modern Satsang movement is based on that model of spiritual experience being called enlightenment. So after your spiritual experience has been officially declared enlightenment by someone who had their spiritual experience declared to be enlightenment by someone else who once flew over Lucknow, you are then urged to teach that to others as being awakening or enlightenment.

Part of the appeal of such a model is that the goal of virtually every seeker is to gain this enlightenment. Therefore, if you tell them that they gained it, because they're getting what they wanted, and they are happy with the teacher for giving it to them. If they're honest and they say, "Well, this enlightenment, this experience that was so profound and important seems to have gone or ebbed," then the teacher says, "Well, it isn't really gone, you're just settling into it. You're just learning your new spiritual body. Your physical being is learning how to accept it" or some similar explanation often accompanied by a supporting quote from a sage who has been dead long enough to no longer be controversial. Implicit in the notion that enlightenment is progressive is that enlightenment is a state - an experiential state. The pointer in this teaching is that it is not an experiential state; an experiential state is by its nature transitory. If you're experiencing something, it will change. The very basis of duality is change. Change is integral to experience. In fact, what we call life is movement and change. In the absence of this movement, when it's localized in an organism, that state is what we call death.

So in terms of the experience of life, the states of life are always alternating, but this is not what is pointed to in this teaching as enlightenment. It is why sages like Nisargadatta Maharaj would speak from the standpoint of Totality and make statements such as, "I'm awake even when I'm asleep. I will live even after I am dead." They are linguistically pointing to that which is not conditional. That which is the source and substance of everything - what we "truly are" - is not experiential except in its aspect. It's experiential only as what we can know and touch and taste and live. But enlightenment is beyond that kind of knowing because it is beyond the limit of experiential knowledge.

With love,

Wayne

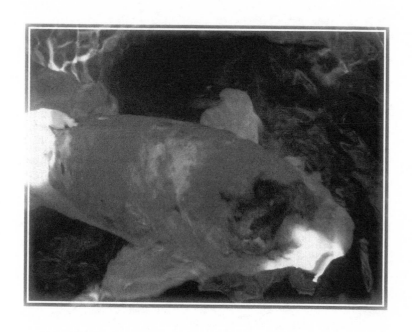

Hello my loves,

As I have been traveling around, there has been a lot of interest lately in Ramesh's concept of the working mind and the thinking mind. The working mind is, as the name suggests, the aspect of the organism that does the work of keeping the organism functioning. It is the repository of genetic heritage, memory, knowledge, culture, identity, all of those qualities that are essential for day to day living. The working mind functions in accordance with its programming. This programming is dynamic; it's an ongoing process whereby new information is being added to the mix all the time.

What Ramesh calls the thinking mind is another term for what is commonly referred to as the ego. The thinking mind's sole function - the ONLY thing it does - is to claim the operation of the working mind as its own doing and become involved in that operation to the extent solely of preserving itself. It's a false claimer of primacy or authorship which arises in virtually every human at the age of about two and a half. The ego/thinking mind authors nothing. There is no such thing as ego-created action.

The body-mind organism that is popularly called a sage is one in which the thinking mind has died. Famous historical resurrections not withstanding, dead is dead and there is no possibility of return. That is my working definition for what constitutes an organism called the sage and what the event of enlightenment represents. It is that very precise occurrence. Therefore, far from being a superman, the sage is completely ordinary. In this model the sage has not gained something more but rather is simply a human organism with one thing LESS... it is without the false sense of personal authorship.

With love,

Wayne

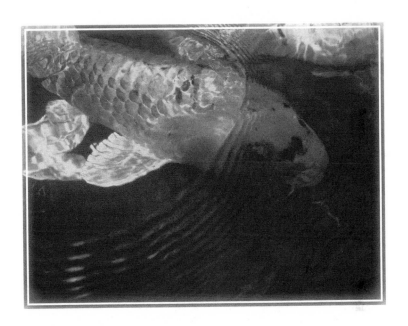

Hello my loves,

The new book Christa and I have been working on for the last year or so arrived today from the printers. It is always amazing for me to hold a new book in my hand...it is not unlike the birth of a child.

Ten years elapsed between my first and second books and then five years between the second and third. I suppose all that means is that it is taking less and less time for me to say Nothing.

In recognition of this I am copying a passage from the book entitled —

GIFTS

If you look back over your life, you will see that the most positive, life-changing events happened unexpectedly. They were like gifts. These milestones in your life were not things you set out to do or get. They came without your planning them, without your working to get them. In fact, if you look very closely, you may realize if you truly had been in control of your life you would have short-changed yourself. You could never have constructed those blessings; you had no idea that they even existed.

Nonetheless, working to get what you think is best is part of what happens. Sometimes you get what you're working for and sometimes you don't. That's part of the process, as well. This Teaching doesn't suggest any particular kind of behavior, either sitting doing nothing or actively pursuing whatever you want.

As Ramesh is quick to point out — "Life is a happening."

With love,

Wayne

Hello my loves,

Many people who come to my Talks say they are there because of an interest in enlightenment. But when we get down to what this thing called enlightenment actually IS, there is enormous confusion.

When I talk about enlightenment, I talk about it very, very specifically, and it's very simple. In humans, at around the age of two-and-a-half, a shift occurs whereby they change from free-flowing, uninvolved beings to experiencing everything in terms of Me! and Mine! It is that moment in which what I call the false sense of personal authorship kicks in. It happens to virtually every human being. It is the false sense that I as this body-mind am the source; that I as this body-mind am responsible for making it all happen.

It is this false sense of personal authorship that creates suffering, because the sense is that I am in control of things, and, yet, there is continuous evidence to the contrary - that I'm not in control. So a powerful tension is established. In some body-minds, for whatever reason, that sense of personal authorship permanently dissolves - dies. That event, for lack of a better name, is called enlightenment. Over the millennia, generations of seekers have mystified the hell out of it. Basically, it's an event that happens in the history of some human organisms.

Now, the reason this event is so interesting to people is that the organism through which it happens is no longer suffering. There is total acceptance within the organism. There is total acceptance because it is understood that what is, is. There is no longer a separate sense of me to become involved with what is and claim it as mine - egoically mine. When that process is no longer occurring, that permanent lack of occurrence may be called peace or bliss or enlightenment. What is crucial to realize is that it is a happening. It happens as part of the functioning of the universe. The pointer of this teaching is that everything happens that way; everything happens as part of the functioning of Totality.

With love,

Wayne

Hello my loves,

When I started my spiritual quest - nineteen years ago or so - I got various books on meditation and began doing Tai Chi and such. I even cobbled together my own meditation. Basically, what I did was get up about 6:30 in the morning and sit quietly on the floor cross-legged, with my back up against a straight surface. I would watch my breath exit the tip of my nose, and I had a mantra that I went through - it was about 10 or 12 words. Each time I went through it I dropped a word, then when I got down to one word I went back up by adding a word on each repetition. I did this most mornings.

One morning I was sitting in meditation and all of a sudden an incredible rush of energy ran right up my spine and out the top of my head. My entire being flooded out the top of my head and started jetting out into the universe. I was sitting there thinking, "Oh, this is good! This is really good!" (I'd done enough drugs in the past to know what to do with an experience like this, so I went with it.) My whole being was expanding out the top of my head and merging with the universe. There was a continuous rush. It was absolutely extraordinary. It was so amazing! I never had a drug experience this good. Compared to any of the psychedelics I had ever done, this was the ultimate! Wow!

After fifteen or twenty minutes, it all settled back down and I was sitting there thinking, "This meditation stuff is great!" So, the next morning I get up at about 6:10. (I figured it wouldn't hurt to start twenty minutes early) I sit back down, settle into the same position and start the mantra.

"Okay, here we go!" I said, urging the energy to begin its movement up my spine. No luck. Every day, for weeks, I was back in that exact same position, and the energy-up-the-spine experience never came back.

I had a similar experience playing golf. I played a hundred and twenty rounds of golf that were crap. Then one day I played six holes in which the ball went precisely where I was aiming, it rolled to the exact spot it was supposed to; everything was perfect. Of course then I started thinking, "What did I just do to make that happen?" and my game went back to crap again.

I no longer feel compelled to sit in formal meditation or to swing a golf club. I am truly blessed.

With love,

Wayne

Hello my loves,

Everything I say is a pointer, a pointer to that which is here, now, in this moment. It's The Great Mystery. It's a great and perpetual mystery because it will never be solved. It is the mystery of life and living, the mystery that is this manifest universe. And no matter how complex our explanations, no matter how elegant our descriptions of 'what is,' they remain hopelessly limited pointers. And the mystery remains.

You have been touched by the mystery. The mystery has its hooks in you. And whether or not you feel good about that depends on the day. But there is something glorious, something wonderful about connecting to the mystery. Once tasted, it will never be forgotten. And so we gather together in this Teaching, not because the truth can be known, but because the truth is inescapable.

The beautiful thing about a mystery is that it engages our attention. Humans are interested in that which they cannot explain. We are curious beings; we want to know, to understand. We're drawn forward by this quality of the unexplained. What the teaching does is point to that which is beyond the apparent mystery, to that which is the source and the substance of everything. Sometimes in a moment of grace there is - what was called by the teacher Wei Wu Wei - apperception. Apperception is knowing without a knower, experiencing without an experiencer, understanding without an understander. The path to that moment of grace is often circuitous, and it may go through some painful or strange places. Ultimately it is all understood to be part of an incredible tapestry of existence, part of the Totality that represents itself as this great mystery.

May your New Year be filled with much peace and joy and love!

With love,

Wayne

Hello my loves,

You want your purveyors of Truth
To look and act special.
You want them different
And separate
And powerful.
You prefer to imagine them
Cloaked in light
Than sitting on the toilet.
You like them passionless, sexless,
Mellow, gentle and kind.
You like the idea of miracles
And will invent them when necessary.
Your strategy is to keep them
Out there
Far away from you
Exotic and mysterious.
You revel in the myth
Of the Enlightened individual
Hoping to someday be so empowered.
What you can't tolerate
Is for them to appear
As ordinary as you.
Ram Tzu know this . . .
You always miss the Truth
Because it is too plain to see.

With love,

Wayne

Hello my loves,

My Dad died last week. It was an extraordinary experience. On Wednesday, March 9 he received the diagnosis of advanced incurable cancer and he made the decision to stop his dialysis treatments and thus spare his family and himself the agony of a painful and prolonged death. I visited him in his home several hours after he had made that decision and what I saw in him was the blessing of total acceptance. He was at peace, without fear or regret. In all my years with him I had never seen him this way before. He had always been in a competition with life, trying to master it and keep it well arranged. As with all of us, sometimes things went his way, sometimes they didn't.

The hospice people came and made all the practical arrangements for things like drugs and a hospital bed. Friends and family members came to say good-bye. Many congratulated my Dad on his courage and fortitude. He smiled back at them benignly, saying softly it was simply a blessing. Many were the protestations that he was being too modest, that he had earned this reward just as he had earned and thus deserved the love of his family. He never argued (totally uncharacteristic of him!) but he never wavered. He knew at the root of his being that it was all Grace...every bit of it.

He lived for four more days and in those four days we shared the most wonderful of unspoken understandings.

Unspoken because there was no need to speak it, just as there were no words adequate to convey it. I looked into my Father's eyes and rejoiced in the profound Absence I found there. I could not wish for any better end to the life of this man I loved. I was glad for him and glad for me.

Life can be so incredibly sweet..........

and so can death.

With much love,

Wayne

Hello my loves,

In our Advaita teaching, one gateway to Insight is the recognition of the mechanistic nature of the body-mind organism with which we are so often identified as the author.

Last week, three articles appeared in the L.A. Times describing scientific discoveries that support the mechanistic approach. The first described how researchers in Vienna have identified the hormone responsible for our making decisions to trust someone or not. After inhaling the hormone spray subjects were significantly more likely to make decisions to trust strangers.

In a second article it was reported that geneticists working with fruit flies were able to identify and manipulate the gene responsible for sexual orientation. After the gene manipulation male fruit flies began exhibiting the sexual patterns distinctive to females.

In a third study on a subject so near and dear to so many of our hearts, scientists at St. Thomas Hospital in London discovered that a woman's ability to have an orgasm was directly linked to her genetic make-up.

It is through questioning the basic assumptions of human existence that insight into our true nature may be realized. One of the most insidious of these basic assumptions is that I (as this body mind organism) am the author of my thoughts, feelings and actions. This Teaching is without dogma or doctrine, its sole function is to ask again and again - IS IT TRUE?

Spiritual teachings and modern scientific research may provide moral support for your conclusions but the real benefit comes from the actual investigation itself.

IS IT TRUE?

In the deep examination of this most fundamental of questions - profound Understanding sometimes results.

With much love,

Wayne

Hello my loves,

I am often asked, "Does everything happen as part of the functioning of Totality or is effort required by the spiritual aspirant?"

Effort by the spiritual aspirant may well be required as part of the functioning of Totality!

As always we must look deeply into the source of the effort. Does the spiritual aspirant have the capacity to author the effort? Or is the spiritual aspirant's actions and ultimately the spiritual aspirant himself part of a larger functioning?

These are the essential questions raised by this Advaita Teaching. But the Teaching does not truly value the answers. It is the investigation itself which is the heart of the Teaching.

It is for this reason that pure Advaita is without doctrine or precepts. The Teaching is humble. It makes no claim on the Truth. It is simply a collection of pointers, encouraging an investigation that ultimately ends in Nothing...the Nothing which we all truly ARE.

With much love,

Wayne

Hello my loves,

Ramesh's latest book landed on my desk a few days ago and I was delighted to see that he is still in top form. Ramesh's Teaching is a living one and thus is constantly in flux. After many years of esoterically emphasizing the illusory nature of the individual his approach has become increasingly down-to-earth and practical. He meets the spiritual seekers at their point of identification and then deftly leads them to deeper understanding. One of the tools Ramesh uses is to challenge the seeker into examining what it is he imagines Enlightenment to be...what are the imagined benefits? So the question ultimately boils down to the new books title: Seeking Enlightenment — Why? I hope this newsletter finds you well and at peace, abiding in the deepest possible conviction that with all of the joys and agonies of the day, the Universe is in perfect order.

With much love,

Wayne

Hello my loves,

Gary Starbuck died a week or so ago. He was a good friend of mine, someone I could sit with for long stretches without feeling the need to talk.

I met Starbuck nearly twenty years ago at one of Ramesh's early Talks in Hollywood, California. He had just come from the mountains of Mexico where he had been prospecting for gold. I'm not sure how we became friends but I am quite sure why — we shared a love and deep respect for Ramesh and his Teaching.

Starbuck later went to Bombay and effectively took up residence on the roof of Ramesh's flat. He stayed several months during which time he extracted hundreds of particularly fine passages from Ramesh's various writings. These were subsequently edited and compiled into one of my favorite Ramesh books — A NET OF JEWELS.

I will spare you a lengthy discourse on how no one is ever born and no one ever dies and how it is all simply a play of Consciousness or an opportunity to know your True Nature and say: He was a fine man and he is missed.

With much love,

Wayne

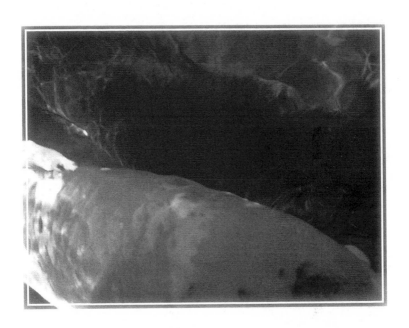

Hello my loves,

The process that's happening in this Advaita is one of inquiry and examination; whereby you gain insight by looking at your own experiences. In the course of life, experiences happen. The question is, what was your part in bringing those experiences into being?

If you look back over your life you will see that people you never knew existed suddenly entered your life and brought with them enormous life changes. They might have been lovers, teachers, enemies or gurus. How could you have brought them into your life, if you didn't even know that they were alive?

Perhaps by looking at your history you will see that events happened in your life that were part of a much larger happening than what you could possibly create with your own physical being. If you can look at your own experience and your own background, you may begin to see that your present state is a product of huge forces outside of your egoic control. This teaching simply directs your attention to look. Insight follows or it does not.

Clearly, if you were in charge - if any of us were in charge and capable of creating our own realities - we'd all be saints! We'd be loving and kind and generous all the time, because when we're loving and kind and generous, we feel better, everybody around us feels better, and this translates into a better life. The fact that despite our best intentions, and our most earnest observations and efforts, we're still filled with positive and negative qualities, seems to suggest a certain lack of control on the part of the organism.

If you look, and you are blessed to be able see the vast universal forces that were operative in creating who you are today, then guilt eases naturally, on its own. You don't have to make any efforts to reduce it; it simply dissipates in the seeing, as you understand that who you are and what you are is a function of the Universe. Both your finer qualities and those qualities that you and others might not like are part of this mixed bag that constitutes every human being.

May this vision grow within you in the coming year.

With love,

Wayne

Hello my loves,

I have recently returned from Mumbai and my annual winter visit to see Ramesh. As always, it was a truly joyous and blessed time. To spend time in the presence of one's guru is life's greatest pleasure.

I am often asked why I continue to visit Ramesh even though there is no longer any "seeking need" to do so. For me, the seeking long ago morphed from a process of acquisition whereby I was hoping to GET something to a state of Acceptance wherein there was not only nothing left to GET but more importantly, no longer an egoic 'me" needing to get IT. What remained was a man named Wayne who loved a little Indian retired banker named Ramesh. For almost twenty years now, that love has flowed unabated. It matters not if we are in the Satsang room together or eating a meal together or watching cricket on television together or simply sitting together in comfortable silence, the love that is the very essence of the guru/disciple relationship is there.

Each year when I visit Ramesh I get to watch with amusement, awe and delight how his Teaching evolves and changes its emphasis. Never wavering from the fundamental Understanding, his approach continues to move and dance like a boxer's. This continued movement keeps the more "advanced" and knowledgeable disciples alert and on their toes.

One of the greatest obstacles to a deepening of Understanding is the complacency inherent in knowing something. Once you have an answer there is no longer any movement. Inquiry is dead. What remains is a dull and lifeless repetition of a concept that may have once brought insight and is now mistaken for insight itself. Ramesh's continual changes keeps his disciples engaged and active. His current emphasis on the value of the Teaching in daily living is simply another door opening into the corridor of Truth.

The value of the guru is not in what you can get from him...it is the guru/disciple relationship itself which is its own reward.

With love,

Wayne

Hello my loves,

Every time it rains, the ants that live under our house are driven up through the walls and into our living space. Today, as I often do, I took a broad swipe at them, killing many. It was a brutal and cold hearted act, one for which I felt absolutely no remorse. It put me in mind of a statement Ramesh made many years ago that affected me deeply. He said, "The Universe is not human-hearted." On that particular day the statement was a revelation...I saw beyond seeing into the unbiased interconnectedness of all things.... the heart of the living paradox.

The notion of God (be it seen as a wise human figure or an impersonal force called Consciousness) is generally associated with benevolence towards humans (except in cases of just punishment for wrongs committed, aka karma). This idea fuels most religions and spiritualities. It echoes in the terms often used for God - "our Father" or "The Beloved". And it is central to the theme that today's humans are the cutting edge of a great evolution/revolution in Consciousness, be it called the Age of Aquarius or something more modern sounding. Is this True or is it simply another human conceit? Does the Universe actually have a preference? If so, what evidence is there that the preference is for humans? It may be useful to examine these questions for yourself.

We can say with some certainty, Wayne is not ant-hearted. Is the Universe human-hearted?

With much love,

Hello my loves,

Jnana (the path of knowledge) and Bhakti (the path of love and gratitude) and Karma (the path of action) are not separate. They never have been. The distinctions are purely notional, not actual. The mind, the heart and the body are bound together as a seamless whole.

I can't tell you how many times I have heard the so-called Knowledge people put down the Heart People for their "slavish devotion to the guru" while the Heart People complain that the Knowledge people are "cold and in their heads." Meanwhile the Action people (when they take a break from being busy) look at the others, shake their heads and wonder why "those people don't get off their butts and DO something!"

It is all just too ridiculous and all too human. People are born with different natures and one of the qualities of having a nature is to feel that it is natural, normal and right. Unfortunately, that often makes people with different natures, unnatural, abnormal and wrong.

The way out of this critical quagmire is through first understanding one's own relative nature, and ultimately Understanding one's True nature. As you begin to see the genetic and environmental forces that continue to combine to shape this body-mind organism that bears your name, you may glimpse the Essence which is the source and the substance of everything.

This Advaita teaching insistently points to that Essence and is available to everyone regardless of who they think they are.

With much love,

Wayne

Hello my loves,

To judge something you need a scale and since everyone has their own scale, judgments of the same thing often vary. The question then becomes, whose scale is RIGHT.

The human mind has a hunger for certainty. It is as if it senses its own inherent limitations and seeks to overcome them with concepts such as Absolute Truth, Absolute Goodness, Absolute Love, Absolute Beauty etc. The traditional method of certifying the RIGHTNESS of these Absolutes is divine revelation, meaning God tells you either directly via a "vision" or a "voice" (with or without "spiritual" drugs and practices) or indirectly via the recorded accounts (scriptures) of someone else's interaction with God.

Modern variants on this theme seek to use scientific or pseudo-scientific methodology to determine the properties of the Absolute, but as with the religious methods agreement is impossible to come by.

There is an inherent arrogance associated with believing you know the Truth. It is the ego's ultimate empowerment.

For me, the beauty of this Teaching is that it does NOT claim to be the Truth. It is simply a collection of pointers. It directs the student to look for him or herself into the Mystery that is the essence of existence. It is often a frightening journey without an Absolute scale by which to measure your progress. In the end, however, the Understanding reveals itself in a humility that is at once transcendent and sublime.

With much love,

Wayne

Hello my loves,

I am just back from spending Guru Purnima in Mumbai with Ramesh and it was completely glorious. I am often asked, "Is a guru necessary?" The question is actually misconceived. It is not that the guru is needed so that the spiritual seeker can get what he is seeking but rather that the guru is among the greatest of the Universe's gifts. Should you be fortunate to receive this amazing gift it is immediately apparent that the relationship with the guru is an end in itself rather than a means to some further objective.

Ramesh at 89 is as strong and as focused in his presentation of the Teaching as he has ever been. As I sit and listen to him it is as if listening to a beloved symphony in which every note is familiar and expected and yet each performance is unique and fresh.

This Guru Purnima was particularly meaningful for me as it marked exactly ten years since that startling day when Ramesh concluded his Guru Purnima talk by saying, "You should all come back tomorrow, tomorrow Wayne will be giving the Talk." In that moment I could never have imagined where the Teaching would carry me....all the towns and cities and countries...all the men and women, old and young, some swelling with new life others preparing to die, all the hearts ready to burst open, all the brows unfurrowed and all the eyes bright with a new Understanding. What a surprise and delight this life is!

I consider myself to be amongst the most fortunate of men, to have found my guru in Ramesh and to have been filled, a most unlikely vessel to carry this magnificent Teaching.

For all of you who have sent donations and gifts and messages on this Guru Purnima, I thank you for your love and support.

With much love,

Wayne

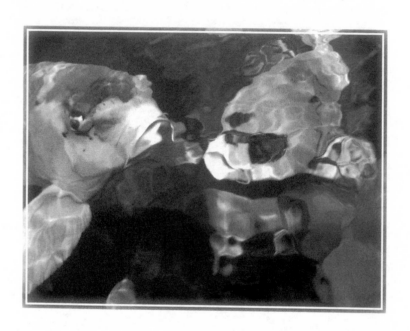

Hello my loves,

One of the most discouraging and unpleasant phases in the evolution of this Understanding is the point at which you find yourself feeling remote and disconnected from all that is happening around you. It as if the world has gone completely grey — nothing is important, nothing hurts particularly badly but nothing feels particularly joyous either. You're not really depressed but you're not really happy — everything has a sameness about it.

Such a condition often coincides with the initial recognition that you are not truly the author of your thoughts, feelings or actions. It is as if the ego, having been exposed for what it ISN'T shifts its involvement into a new gear. No longer able to claim to be the author it now poutingly claims that there is nothing worth authoring. Yes, it is another lie but it is a persuasive one. As with the previous lie, the lie of personal authorship, a possible solution is to fix it in the bright light of inquiry. Is it true? Is the appearance the reality?

Eventually the clouds disperse and the greyness goes with it. The landscape of life is once again illuminated in all its beauty and all its ugliness...all its joys and all its sorrows...what is seen is what has always been there...an infinite, fantastic diversity.

With much love,

Wayne

Hello my loves,

The term "Consciousness" is used in this teaching to point to That which is EVERYTHING and at the same time is not a thing. Other popular and equivalent terms are Source, God, Unicity, Tao and Absolute (to name but a few).

Since everything that is manifest is Consciousness, nothing can be higher/lower Consciousness or more/less Consciousness. If we say all oceans are water, it is meaningless to say the Pacific Ocean is more water than the Atlantic Ocean. We can say one ocean is bigger or smaller or saltier than another but their essential nature, their waterness, is the same.

All too often, God, the Absolute, Consciousness is invoked as a relative standard. One group claims to know either through faith or "science" what is more "Godly" but ALWAYS some other group is there to disagree.

The human mind via its senses is designed to make distinctions between things. It compares and analyzes. In fact, all of humankind's collected knowledge is the product of comparisons, in which the newly "discovered" is added as an extension or revision to what was previously "known." Thus human knowledge is based entirely on differences and similarities. As man seeks to know God it is only natural for him to try to use familiar tools and methods. Unfortunately, these tools and methods only work at knowing the material/relative aspects of Consciousness (the manifest world) they are worthless for knowing Consciousness as the Absolute.

This is where we enter the realm of the mystic. Knowledge and science and even faith have to be discarded. This is the world of the transcendent. It is here that the distinction between the knower and the known fades away. It is here that all words are useless. It is here that everything stops.

With much love,

Wayne

Hello my loves,

I am not a Buddhist, nor a Hindu nor a Jew. Not much of a humanist either. In fact, other than tall, fat and bald, I would be hard pressed to say exactly what I am. Of course, I am not tall compared to most pro basketball players; and compared to some of the people I see on the beach, I'm not all that fat either; and I do have more hair than a lot of men...and that sort of sums up the problem inherent in labels.

Labels, like all knowledge available to the human organism, are based on comparisons, and comparisons are all about context, and context keeps changing. Nothing is fixed. Everything keeps moving around. It is enough to drive you crazy. Just when you thought you knew something, someone comes along and rearranges things, and that dreaded uncertainty slides right back in again. This is both the good and the bad news. With uncertainty comes insecurity, and insecurity causes agitation, and agitation moves things around. Movement is the basis of change and change means life.

I am a big proponent of LIFE. In fact, I am such a big proponent of LIFE that when people come to me and ask me what they should do, I generally advise them to breathe. They often assume that this answer means I did not understand their question and so they explain further - "No, breathing happens independent of me, I want to know what I should do."

So the question for today is: What DOESN'T happen independent of you?

And while you are pondering that, don't forget to breathe.

With much love,

Wayne

Hello my loves,

Here's to life lived by humans!

As a student of non-duality you have undoubtedly been seduced or brow-beaten into acknowledging that you don't exist. Unfortunately, like the pointers from so many teachings (mine included) the essence of what is being pointed at is often obscured by dull-witted literalism.

The Truth ALWAYS lies beyond the knowable and speakable. When a teacher says or writes something he is directing your attention into the middle-distance - that space that is neither here nor there...referenceless, undefined. The challenge is that your entire physical/mental being revolts from this. You instinctively seek solidity and reference - the solace of the known.

Know that this is divinity expressing as humanity - a cosmic game of hide and seek played out by You and through you.

What could possibly be more wondrous? What could possibly be more awe-inspiring? Life and living as it happens in this eternal moment.

With much love,

Wayne

Hello my loves,

Spiritual pride takes many forms. Some are gross and obvious, others are more subtle and hidden. Regardless of the form, spiritual pride has its roots in the belief that "I" know the Truth.

Our Teaching does not advise you to rid yourself of spiritual pride, rather it directs you to look at the belief that fuels the pride. Is Truth (in the Absolute sense) knowable?

As transcendent Understanding deepens, belief in the certainty of knowable truth lessens and a simple humility prevails. You find yourself less critical of the convictions and practices of others. You become content to know what you know and believe what you believe without being burdened by the crushing weight of relative knowledge masquerading as Absolute Truth.

As this new year dawns before us, perhaps you will take a moment to reflect on what is True?

Insight may await you.

With much love,

Wayne

Hello my loves,

You have every right to be suspicious of what I teach... after all there is much bullshit about, most of it innocuous enough but some quite insidious.

However, it is not enough to merely be suspicious of me. That is too easy. You must have the courage to be suspicious of yourself... of those things you hold to be True. Could it not be possible that you are mistaken in your most fundamental assumptions? Is it not possible that you could be wrong? The mere acknowledgment of this is the seed of genuine humility.

I hope you will be thorough in investigating whatever is said here and fearless in looking at what you assume to be true. Such considerations may well lead you to the door of your True Self.

With much love,

Wayne

Hello my loves,

Nothing gives me greater pleasure than to see this Teaching find a home in someone. It is like watching a flower bloom in the spring. To see the furrows relax between someone's eyebrows, to watch their shoulders drop as their tension fades, to see a smile creep onto their lips and the light begin to radiate from their eyes is for me, a thing of surpassing beauty. I notice it happening in nearly every gathering and I am awed by the incredible power of the Teaching.

Several years ago, Ramesh began to emphasize the impact of the realization of the Teaching in daily life rather than talking about the esoteric and the philosophical. It upset a lot of his devotees who had grown comfortable and complacent in the belief that they KNEW Ramesh's Teaching. But I thought it was great fun! A true Master shakes things up. He keeps the Teaching vibrant and alive by changing the presentation...because after all, life IS change.

This is a Living Teaching! It connects to who you are and what you are RIGHT NOW...in THIS moment. It challenges you and nurtures you. It is at once impossibly difficult and supremely easy. It forces you to work very, very hard but it does all the work itself.

We are truly blessed to have such a Teaching!

With much love,

Wayne

Hello my loves,

If you are reading this you are part of the world of spiritual inquiry. You may consider yourself a seeker or you may consider yourself as having already found or you may consider yourself no one at all. The fact is...you are reading this! (or if you consider yourself no one, then let it be said.... there is reading happening!) The importance of this is that it points to the fact that there is SOMETHING.

That SOMETHING exists regardless of your opinion about it. It exists regardless of your beliefs or your philosophy. That SOMETHING is the one, indisputable Truth. It is the start point and the end point of all spiritual knowledge.

This Living Teaching points you to this moment in life.... here....now.... to the essential and indisputable. In the total recognition of this, there is no where to go and nothing to get...in the absence of this recognition the Living Teaching may be of interest.

Interest for whom?

Interest to what end?

Welcome to the Living Teaching.

With much love,

Wayne

Hello my loves,

My beloved Ramesh, will celebrate his 90th birthday in a few days and if the gods cooperate I will be there in Mumbai to help honor the day. Nothing could give me greater pleasure. I consider myself to be infinitely blessed to have been give this connection with the man I call my guru.

When I first met Ramesh I was not looking for a guru. In fact, I didn't consider myself to be the sort of person to 'subjugate' myself to someone else. I subscribed to the notion that we are all equal and thus relationships such as guru and disciple struck me as antiquated and if truth be told, a bit cultish.

But I was to learn that the guru/disciple relationship is about love and devotion....not subjugation. The guru asks for nothing and gives everything in return. The disciple gives what he can and with grace, as time goes on, asks for less and less.

In the twenty years I have been privileged to be connected to Ramesh he has given me more than I could ever hope to repay. I consider it a blessing to have been able to help support him financially and to have in some small way contributed to facilitating his Teaching. Whatever I have done has been done without obligation or demand either by Ramesh or by me. I suppose you could say it is love in action.

Some of you reading this already know the unmitigated joy of having found your guru. For those of you who have not yet had this pleasure...know that life is full of surprises... anything can happen!

With much love,

Wayne

Hello my loves,

I was recently asked, "What is your philosophy of life?"
My immediate response was - "Breathe"
The questioner assumed from this response that I had
misunderstood her question so she repeated it a little
differently - "What do you think is the best way to live?"
she asked.

"BREATHE!" I repeated.

Everyone laughed but I was not making a joke. I have
no interest in philosophy or spirituality as an intellectual
chess game. To my mind, a philosophy of life must be
completely practical - it must have meaning in the office
and the bedroom, the church and the night club. Thus, the
Living Teaching is pointing to this most basic of human
functions - to live is to breathe. But everyone knows they
are not the creators or even the masters of their breath, it
literally has a life of its own. And since the breath is (except
for certain yogic practices) immune from the claims of the
ego, it is generally of little interest. It is JUST there.

The Living Teaching proposes a look with fresh eyes
at this breath that is living us, animating us, giving us the
power of choice, thought, feeling and action. This breath is
an open invitation to the reality of What IS...perhaps you
will find that this is the moment you walk through.

With much love,

Wayne

Hello my loves,

There is so much fear in the world...and no wonder. Every day we are bombarded with reports of wars, murders, thefts, rapes, environmental destructions and misconduct at every level of society.

Certain "fears" are warranted and healthy...if nothing is done to reverse the course, our children or our children's children will likely be extinguished by the pollutants in our environment. If we put our hand through the fence against which the pit bull is hurling himself to get at us we will likely be mauled. These are practical or functional fears. But there is a whole other level of fear and this has very little to do with the practical or the functional. This is the fear that is the product of involvement by the ego. This is the fear of what will become of "ME." This is the fear that is experienced as suffering.

The human organism is ultimately quite fragile and the number of tragedies that could potentially befall it is limitless. The ego that falsely claims to be in control of things is revealed as powerless in the face of this list of possible ills. The product of this interface between the ego's claim of power and the evidence of actual powerlessness (as seen and read daily in the news) is fear. The response to this that we see most often is to try to get MORE control. The latest incarnation of this attempt is the hugely popular program called The Secret. Such schemes feed the egos insatiable need for the thing it most sorely lacks...power.

The Living Teaching takes an entirely different approach to this phenomenon of egoic fear. It points to the root cause of the fear itself. It helps expose the fundamental falseness of the egoic claim. Thus, it is not likely to be popular nor mainstream. However, it CAN BE incredibly effective in helping to reduce the strength of the false claim and thus effective in reducing the resultant fear. As the fear is reduced, the need to hold-on and to control the uncontrollable is reduced and there is less suffering.

With Grace, anything is possible.

With much love,

Wayne

Hello my loves,

"Those who hear not the music
Think the dancers mad"

This should not come as news to those drawn to Advaita. You have discovered an entirely new way of looking at things. Insights have come and you can never go back to the old way of seeing. Your head is in the tigers mouth!

You may have also discovered that talking about these insights puts you at odds with those around you. To even remotely suggest that the individual is not the ultimate source of his actions (and is thus not responsible for creating them) is to invite powerful, sometimes violent opposition. It is as if the world has an unwritten agreement to not look at its most basic assumptions and if you violate that agreement you are in for a rough time.

Nisargadatta Maharaj (my guru's guru) had a strict policy that his disciples were not to discuss the Teaching outside of the Satsang room. Not only did this have the effect of keeping the blind from leading the blind but it helped protect the fragile seedling of the new insight from being trampled by an ego-centric society. While it is not my nature to create policy, I am sympathetic to the spirit of Maharaj's injunction.

The deepening of understanding and the relief from suffering that comes with a weakening of egoic involvement are usually part of a process. In the early stages particularly, it is best to let the Teaching grow strong inside you before taking it out and parading it on the street. You may even find that as the understanding deepens there is an ever lessening impulse to talk about the Teaching at all.

With Grace, everything is possible.

With much love,

Wayne

Hello my loves,

I am periodically taken to task for not having a teaching style more like some of my preceptors - most notably, Nisargadatta Maharaj. Maharaj was famous for speaking from the standpoint of the Absolute. He would say things such as, "I was never born and I will never die" and "I am awake even when I am asleep." Such assertively non-dual statements sometimes had the effect of shocking his listeners into a profound, transcendent Seeing.

I am sympathetic to this approach, but I have rarely been comfortable using it. I feel much more at home when I am meeting my listeners where THEY are... most of them believing that they were born and will die and that they are asleep while asleep. From this point of "obvious" truth we can then proceed to examine the more profound, underlying nature of this "one" who lives and dies and sleeps.

No one can deny that there is EXISTENCE here. The nature of that EXISTENCE can (and has been) debated endlessly. But this EXISTENCE is self-proving. It is not a philosophical debating point but a self-affirming Truth. It is here at the center when you pull off the onion-like layers of your apparent self - the self that lives and dies and sleeps and wakes.

We are the victims of our beliefs. When you "believe" the pointers of a teacher such as Maharaj, the inevitable result is a kind of nihilism in which all that is apparent (including yourself) is denied as meaningless and illusory. When you believe the pointers of a teacher such as myself, the inevitable result is the sense of having a progressively deeper and truer knowledge about the nature of Existence. All such beliefs are equally True and equally false.

So pick your poison. With a little luck...either one will kill the "you" that believes it has found the Truth.

With much love,

Wayne

Hello my loves,

The only requirement for participation in the Living Teaching is that you be Living. If you are convinced you don't exist and therefore are not alive, please feel free to come back later when that wears off. For all the rest of you, welcome!

This aliveness we are talking about is worth investigating. It is here, in this moment. It is as close to you as your breath. In fact, your breath IS this Livingness. You do not have to remember to breathe; your breath is literally breathing you. Stop reading the words on this page for a moment and investigate this phenomenon of breathing....

(If you did not stop, but simply read on to this sentence, I fully understand - you are a lot like me - however, there REALLY is something to be seen in the stopping for a moment, even if you are an "advanced" student and have examined your breath many times previously)

Perhaps you were able to see the way in which your breath "just happens." You breathe even when you forget to breathe. There is a force here that operates independently of your decisions and intentions. It is this force that the Living Teaching is concerned with. It is this Life that is living you - even to the extent that you falsely believe yourself to be living IT.

I am continuously amazed and delighted at the way in which this livingness happens. It is the fuel of miracles, not the least of which is our sharing this thought together! I write: you read. Through an infinitely complex net of relationships there is a kind of recognition, a touching, in which time dissolves and the Unity is revealed.

With much love,

Wayne

Hello my loves,

For those of us who remain so spiritually backward that time and space still exist for us, another year is drawing to a close. It is an opportunity to stop for a moment and reflect on the miracle that is this Livingness. Within the Livingness are the polaric opposites... birth and death, joy and sorrow, pleasure and pain, inhalation and exhalation... and it is the continuous movement between the polarities that is the EXPERIENCE of being alive. Some people believe that death is the end of the Living, when in fact death is simply the end of a particular experience within the Livingness. The Livingness continues even after a particular point of experience is extinguished.

When birth and death are known for what they are — linked opposites within the Livingness — much of the fear and drama drain out of the process.

Sometimes this Living Teaching facilitates an extraordinary insight:

What you TRULY are is not limited to a particular point of experience. What you TRULY are is the Livingness itself.

Happy New Year to ALL!

With much love,

Wayne

Hello my loves,

"Who Cares?" was the title of one of Ramesh's earlier books. This can be understood on two levels. On the surface level, the slang expression indicates a lack of concern or a carefree attitude. While everyone has moments of not caring, even the most god-crazed sadhu will have moments of caring about something.

Which brings us to the deeper meaning in "Who Cares?" Where there IS caring, who produces it? Do you as an individual body-mind mechanism have the capacity to create caring? Certainly you may choose to start or stop caring about something but can you always make your choice happen? If you find you can't always make your choice happen, then that would suggest that some LIVING FORCE other than the egoic "you" determines what happens. It is this LIVING FORCE that Advaita is concerned with and it was with the hope of helping you discover this LIVING FORCE that Ramesh asked "Who Cares?"

With much love,

Wayne

Hello my loves,

You have probably spent your whole life trying to control and modify the events you see are connected to your guilt and suffering. You try to be more patient, more honest, more loving, more chaste, more generous, more open, more tolerant, more productive or more effective. Despite your efforts it is likely that some, perhaps many of the events connected to your suffering and guilt continue to occur.

Now may be the moment for you to take a radically different approach. Rather than trying even harder to control your behavior, perhaps it is time to turn your attention to this OTHER aspect of your sense of guilt and suffering.

The Living Teaching invites you to stop here and take a fresh look at something. Look deeply into the assumption that you COULD have acted/reacted differently in the moment that you did what you did. Examine the claim by the ego that you were the author (the independent source) of that event for which there is now a feeling of guilt.

Is it true?

Is it really true?

Could it have been different?

Were you the independent source of it?

Look deeply.

If you don't see, look again.

With much love,

Wayne

Hello my loves,

This Living Teaching is right here, right now. It is, in fact, as close to you as your breath. When you look deeply into yourself you may be able to see that there is, in this moment, a quality of aliveness that is animating you that is not philosophical and is not abstract. It's there! It is coursing the blood through your veins, it is animating your breath, it is what makes it possible for you to think and speak and see and hear.

This is something that is essential and fundamental and true. It's independent of what you think about it, what you believe about it and what you feel about it. It is here, and with Grace you dissolve into it. You recognize your true self in it. It is this living force, this animating force that has manifested into the complexity we call Life. It is this living force that has manifested into this being which you call yourself.

It is at once wondrous and simply obvious.

With much love,

Wayne

Hello my loves,

Is there something you have done that up to that moment you swore you would never do? Perhaps it was something as simple as wagging your finger in the face of your child (an action your mother did to you and that you promised yourself you would never do to your own child). Or perhaps you had an extra-marital affair despite believing such behavior was wrong. If you examine the history of your life you may recall several such "embarrassments". How is that you did these things that you were adamant that you would never do?

The usual, surface claim of the ego is that "I-the-ego" was responsible. "I" could have and should have done better. "I" should have resisted the temptation. "I" should have been stronger, wiser. "I" should have been less self-centered, less selfish.

The Living Teaching encourages you to look deeply into these actions. Such events can serve as windows into the Truth of what was functioning in those moments. What Universal (non-egoic) forces might have been at work to produce the action in question? Genes? Hormones? Conditioning? Can you begin to isolate any of the influences?

By looking, there may be seeing. In seeing, there may be Understanding.

With much love,

Hello my loves,

I am sorry to have to report that our dear Ramesh had surgery on his gallbladder a little more than a week ago. I am delighted to report that the surgery was successful and he is well on the road to recovery. As of this writing (June 21) he is scheduled to be out of the hospital in a day or two. He will then begin a period of convalescence at home. His daily Talks in his home will resume as soon as he has recovered sufficiently. Knowing Ramesh, he will be sitting in his chair, talking to visitors about Advaita long before his doctors and his family think he should...such is the passion for the Teaching that burns within him.

We will post details about the resumption of his talks in the EVENTS CALENDAR section of the advaita.org website as they become available.

Such events remind us of what a precious resource we are blessed to have in the person of Ramesh. His kindness, wisdom and generosity of spirit are amazing gifts to all who have the good fortune to meet him. I am sure you will join with me in wishing him a speedy recovery.

With much love,

Wayne

Hello my loves,

One of my favorite quotes is: "Life is like licking honey off a thorn." It points to those twin qualities that make up all of existence. There is no pleasure without pain, no joy without sorrow. To deeply realize this is to come into harmony with What Is.

Ramesh's words in this month's newsletter (look towards the end, below) point to the fact that this deep realization comes from a "bold, clear look" into the Essence. One of the most direct avenues into this looking is to start with what is there in front of you....your experience of the moment, your breathing, your sense of aliveness....any of these will do. If you find yourself spinning off into philosophical speculation....what does it mean? why is it happening?... come gently back to the experience in front of you.

With Grace comes a dissolution of the Problem of Life leaving an unobstructed view of life's ongoing problems and joys.

With much love,

Wayne

Hello my loves,

This Teaching encourages you to find the truth for yourself, by looking into your own experience. In the course of your life, experiences happen. The real question is, what was your part in bringing those experiences into being? If you deconstruct any event in your life you may begin to see that any singular event is part of a much larger and more complex matrix than what you could possibly create with your own physical being. If you can look at your own experience and your own background, you may begin to see that how you are in this moment is a product of vast genetic and environmental forces beyond the possibility of personal control.

If you look, and you see that these Universal life forces were responsible for creating who you are today, then guilt eases naturally, on it's own. You don't have to make any efforts to reduce it; it simply dissipates in the seeing.

We're all a mixed bag of qualities. If any of us were capable of creating our own realities we would all be saints! We would be loving and kind and generous all the time, because when we're loving and kind and generous, we feel better, everybody feels better, and it brings more joy into life. The fact that despite our best intentions, and our most earnest observations and efforts, we're still filled with positive and negative qualities, seems to suggest a certain lack of control on the part of the human organism. Perhaps if you look, you will see deeply into the mystery and be freed. I hope so!

With much love,

Wayne

Hello my loves,

The key to The Living Teaching is having a vibrant sense of curiosity. Curiosity is what moves you to look. And sometimes when you look... you see.

I am not telling you you SHOULD be curious. Rather that curiosity already exists inside you. It is what propels you to read these words. It is what brought you to this Teaching.

What is so wonderful about curiosity is that it is without goal and without agenda. Curiosity's sole purpose is to satisfy itself. The wonderful paradox is that curiosity is never truly satisfied. It simply moves focus, going from one thing to another....sometimes deeply, sometimes merely skimming over the surface.

Curiosity is free from the sense that I am doing it. Curiosity is something that simply arises. It is thus freer and more open in scope than formal inquiry. No one has ever failed at curiosity.

The Living Teaching exists to support this curiosity wherever and whenever it arises. It is here to fan the spark in the hope that the spark will eventually become a blaze.... and consume you.

With much love,

Wayne

Hello my loves,

I was watching a new DVD of Nisargadatta with fascination. I felt a resonance with him that I had never felt with any of his pictures or books.

The questions put to him are essentially the same as those put to Ramesh and to me and to most other teachers in this tradition. The questions often have to do with the nature of the Sage and Enlightenment and inevitably they focus on the body-mind organism. Does the Sage worry? Is the Sage afraid of death? Does the Sage acquire Karma? Nisargadatta had little patience with such questions, particularly towards the end of his life when his energy was fading. The thrust of his teaching was away from the body-mind and back to the Self that is the essence of all. He was relentless in his focus on the Absolute rather than the temporal. "What were you before you were conceived?" he asked.

I was particularly amused when in one scene in the DVD Maharaj talked about the LIFE FORCE being responsible for everything. What was written in the subtitle was that the LIGHT SOURCE was responsible for everything! It was certainly a simple and understandable mistake but it illustrates the inherent danger of considering the recorded statements of the guru as being Truth. I would not be surprised to learn that somewhere in the world there was a seeker earnestly prostrating himself in front of a light bulb!

With much love,

Wayne

Hello my loves,

At the end of this newsletter is a wonderful excerpt from Ramesh's unpublished 1989 tour notes about trust.

What he is saying is that trust is essential for living. Without a very fundamental trust we are paralyzed. Normally we think of trust as a faith that someone will act in a manner consistent with our expectations, but the trust Ramesh is pointing to goes far beyond this. The trust he is talking about is a sense that the universe is in perfect order; that even evil, misfortune, illness and betrayal are part of the perfect order of things. To trust in this way is to walk lightly on the earth. It is to know serenity in the midst of calamity. It is to feel comfortable being alive.

The Living Teaching points to the Unity that is all things. It encompasses all that is considered to be good and all that is considered to be bad. It encourages you to look beyond the surface and so know the Truth. Once you see beyond the false claim of being a separate, authoring entity, you will come face-to-face with the Mystery that is the very basis of trust and ultimately of freedom.

With much love and best wishes for 2009,

Wayne

A LIVING GEM FROM RAMESH

The sage, the wise man, has the basic working and living attitude of respectful trust towards nature and human nature, despite wars, revolutions, starvations, floods, rising crime and all manner of horrors. He is not concerned with the notion of original sin, nor does he have the feeling that existence (samsara) is itself a disaster. His basic understanding has the premise that if you cannot trust nature and other people, you cannot trust yourself; if you cannot trust yourself, how can you trust your mistrust of yourself? In other words, without this underlying trust, the faith in the functioning of Totality, the whole system of nature, you are simply paralyzed. Ultimately, of course, it is not really a matter of you on the one hand, trusting nature on the other; it is really a matter of realizing that we and nature are one and the same process, and not separate entities.

1989 (unpublished)

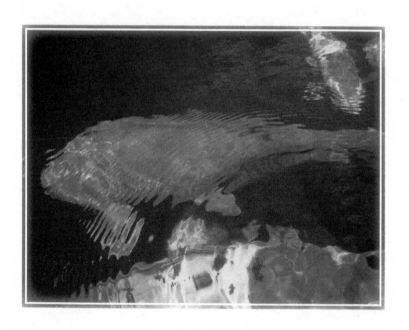

Hello my loves,

The Living Teaching is built on the principle of looking deeply. True Faith is understood to be sighted rather than believed. It arises naturally out of the Understanding of the nature of What Is. Within the Living Teaching, faith and Acceptance are bound together. Whatever you look deeply into may lead you to confront the Mystery that lies at the root of everything. Faith is the profound Understanding of what truly Is.

Deep looking happens through a variety of channels. People we call Thinkers, look primarily with their intellects. People we call Feelers look primarily with their hearts. People we call Doers, look primarily thorough their deeds. People we call Yogis look primarily through their breath and bodies. The Living Teaching embraces and enfolds all these channels. The Living Teaching can be understood as the river from which all the separate channels break off and to which all the separate channels inevitably return.

With love,

Wayne

Hello my loves,

Freedom is a word that is often used interchangeably with the word Enlightenment. To be enlightened is to be free. But have you ever stopped to consider what it means to be free? It is curious. Ask people what they think of when they think of freedom and most people speak in terms of freedom to do what they please. Freedom to go where they want to go. Freedom to say what they want to say and do what they want to do. Freedom is often associated with choice. Freedom to chose a leader (vote). Freedom to chose a spouse. Freedom to chose a career. Boil it down and this kind of freedom is about getting what you want. Presumably, the freer you are, the better able you will be to get what you want and the more satisfied you will be. Such a notion of freedom is inevitably linked to power. If you have physical power you are then free to climb mountains you could not if you are weak. If you have financial power you are free to go places and acquire things you cannot not if you are poor. In this way freedom becomes associated with acquisition or control and so it is that most people imagine that the road to freedom lies in acquisition or control. But the desire for such freedom is limitless and insatiable. The more you get, the more remains ungotten.

We need only read the newspapers to see where such an approach has lead in the fiscal world. In the spiritual world this same desire for acquisition and control takes the form of a spiritual materialism in which more and deeper

UNDERSTANDING is sought. Spiritual freedom is often thought to be freedom from mentation or freedom from anger or freedom from desire. In this way, equanimity and peacefulness are seen as states to be attained either through diligence or surrender.

In fact, freedom is never attained. It can only be revealed. Freedom is not a thing to be acquired but a condition that currently exists. It is here, now and it underlies everything. True freedom is total Acceptance.

With much love,

Wayne

Hello my loves,

Our language can tell us a lot about the assumptions of the society in which we live.

I often hear people say, "I made some bad choices that put me in the bad position I am in now."

On the surface this may seem obvious and indisputable, but it introduces a bigger question. What was the source of the choice?

In children it is clearer. If you ask a young child, "Why did you chose to hit Billy and take away his toy?" the child will look at you blankly. He cannot relate to the notion that he "chose" to do what he did. In his mind, he just DID what he did. If pressed, he will explain it by saying, "I don't know, I just felt like doing it." Simply put, it was a happening. It HAPPENED.

As we grow older, we learn to play the adult game. We learn how to tell elaborate stories about what happens. We learn to give REASONS for what happens. We learn to take credit and blame, which quickly morphs into pride and guilt. At the root of the adult game is the claim of personal authorship, a claim that is deeply rooted in human culture and society. These deep roots are the greatest barrier to an open and unbiased investigation into the truth or falsity of the claim of personal authorship.

The Living Teaching encourages you to be tireless in your pursuit of the truth of What Is. If you find yourself curious and able to look more deeply into the Source, you have been touched in a way that is rare indeed.

With much love,

Wayne

Hello my loves,

> "Believe those who are seeking the truth.
> Doubt those who find it."
>> - Andre Gide (1869-1951)

I am very pleased to have my new book, "Enlightenment Is Not What You Think", coming out this month. If it is at all successful in dispelling some of the myths about Enlightenment, I will be gratified.

In the Living Teaching it is recognized that seeking Truth is infinitely more valuable than finding it. The search is alive and vibrant. Once you think you have found it, the resulting knowledge is but a dead carcass.

Knowledge is acquired. Truth is revealed. The nature of this revelation is an absence rather than a thing that is to be gained. Of course, it is impossible to describe an absence...we can only describe something that has properties. The impossibility of the task of describing Enlightenment, combined with the insatiable thirst on the part of seekers to know what it is, has produced an incredible array of pointers. The inevitable fate of such pointers is that people hear them as descriptions and then take them to be Truths.

It would be an endless and thankless task trying to point out the falacy in each belief about Enlightenment. I have contented myself with presenting a broader perspective on the subject, in which a new and deeper insight may be found. I hope you find it valuable.

As always, we shall see what happens.

With much love,

Wayne

Hello my loves,

About a week before I reached Mumbai for Guru Purnima, I received the sad news that Ramesh's wonderful wife, Sharda had died quietly and peacefully in their home.

What I will always remember about Sharda Balsekar is her hands. They exist, frozen in my memory, fingertips and thumbtip gathered into a point, suspended over a plate of puri batata, as if sprinkling magic, fairy dust. And it WAS a sort of magic, fairy dust...if you can call love, magic, fairy dust. Because that is exactly the ingredient that transformed those mundane componenents into something truly sublime. Sharda's love infused everything and everyone she touched, transforming us and enriching us.

Sharda lived in my home and I lived in hers. For twenty-one years our paths crossed yearly, sometimes briefly, sometimes for months. She was always the epitome of graciousness and subtlety. She was both interesting and interested. She had the ability to make me feel as if I had her complete attention.

Another image that will remain fixed in my mind is of her standing high on the slopes of Mt. Haleakala on the Hawaiian Island of Maui, sipping giddily from a glass of champagne, the helicopter that had brought us there standing ready in the background. Her eyes sparkled like the wine and I could see that in that moment she was truly,

truly happy, almost like a little girl who had been granted a forbidden pleasure.

More than anything...Sharda cared. She cared for her family and for mine. She cared for me and for all of us who were graced with a little of her time here on Earth.

With much love,

Wayne

Hello my loves,

The recent death of Ramesh's dear wife, Sharda, Ramesh's current, serious medical situation (he is in the hospital with pneumonia) and the birth of my first grandchild, Hailey, two weeks ago has gotten me reflecting on this bittersweet miracle of life.

In the Living Teaching, we talk about Life as we experience it as being the sum of birth plus death. As an equation: Birth + Death = Life. This is a very different approach than the common idea that death cancels out life. Life - Death = 0. Death in this model is seen as a negation. It's result is an emptiness, a zero.

When we take the former, holistic approach, death is understood to be an essential component in the formula of Life. Life itself is eternal. Life is the source of everything. It is our enduring, essential nature.

As human beings, birth is usually associated with joy and happiness, death is usually associated with pain and sorrow. I reacted with an almost ecstatic pleasure when I first held my minutes-old granddaughter in my arms. I was later asked how this differed from first holding my daughter in my arms...upon some reflection I realized that my granddaughters birth was more powerful for me because of my present relationship with death. Thirty years ago, when my daughter was born, I had little connection with death. It was an abstraction, something that I was independent of. I intellectually knew I would die some day but there was no reality to it. This is no longer the case. Death is real for me now. I held my Father as he died. I can feel my own mortality in my body as it ages. I have sadly watched my beloved guru grow old and weaken. In a strange but wonderful way this acquaintance with death makes birth all the more spectacular. Birth and death feed each other. In the seeing of this....in the Acceptance that such seeing embodies, there is Peace. May it find you now!

With much love,

Wayne

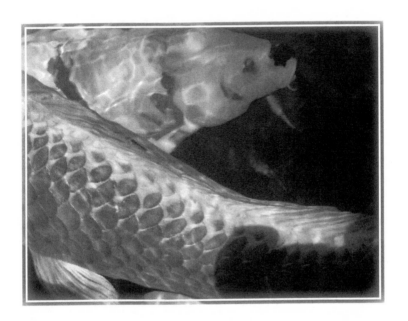

Hello my loves,

One of the most common responses I get during my talks about the Living Teaching is, "If everything is 'just' a happening and is predetermined why should I make any effort to do anything?"

The key word in the statement is "should." In fact, there is truly no question of should. Whether you realize it or not, you do what you do because the Universe dictates your actions. It does so via a combination of genetic predisposition combined with subsequent environmental conditioning (experience and learning). If you look deeply into your own actions you may see that you do things regardless of your feelings that you should or shouldn't do them. The "should" is simply a story that is told about what will happen or has happened. When what happens is aligned with your feeling of "should" you are content. Other times there is a disconnect between what has happened and what you feel "should" have happened and there is guilt (if it is YOU that should have done it differently) or a feeling that the world is messed up (if it is the UNIVERSE that should have done it differently).

At the end of this newsletter is a twenty year old quote from Ramesh in which he talks about effortless effort. What he is describing is effort without the subsequent "should" which is always a product of involvement by the False Sense of Authorship (the "me").

Consider this note as encouragement to continue to follow your curious heart into a place of silent witnessing.

With much love,
Wayne

Dear Friends,

It is with the heaviest of hearts I write to tell you of the passing of our beloved Ramesh this morning at 9 AM in his home in Bombay.

Ramesh was truly an extraordinary being. His life as a successful banker, author and spiritual teacher directly enriched the lives of tens of thousands of people.

Having met Ramesh was one of the defining moments of my life, as I am certain it was for many of you reading this note. His generous spirit, open, loving presence and spiritual Understanding combined to make him one of the truly great Sages of the 20th century. We are truly blessed to have known him...be it "in person" or through his Teaching.

Ramesh lives on. Though his body will this afternoon return to the elements, his spirit lives on in his books and in the hearts of all of us who have known him and loved him..

Twenty-two years ago Ramesh came into my life. Today his body leaves it. To have been able to walk beside him for all this time and to have been able to bow at his feet has been for me the greatest of life's blessings. I shall miss not being able to sit with Ramesh, to watch a cricket match together or to share some chocolate or to laugh at some silly joke he reads from the newspaper. It is not the greatness of the man I will miss most...his greatness remains undiminished by his death...it is the little things, the human things..

Many of you will share with me the exquisite human pain of the loss of a beloved one. If you take a moment to quietly look at it you may see in the pain the wonder of Life itself. If so, it will truly be the Grace of The Guru.

With much love,

Wayne

Hello my loves,

It has been a month now since the death of Ramesh. For me the sharp pain of loss has been replaced by a dull ache. I have received many very beautiful letters and emails from people expressing their love for Ramesh and talking about the profound impact he had on their lives. He was for so many of us one of life's most amazing gifts.

Ramesh used to tell the story of a publisher friend of his who had mistakenly considered himself to be enlightened. When this man's wife died he was consumed with grief and that confused him. He had imagined that he was "above" such mundane, human emotions...that since he knew himself and all things to be the Absolute, who would be left to grieve for who? This points to one of the most persistent myths surrounding enlightenment....that it results in a kind of passive indifference in which all is known to be illusory, including the one who would know it. Most organized religions exhalt the renunciant, the wandering sufi or sadhu or penitent or monk who gives up business and family life to focus on the Supreme. The assumption here is that daily life and the Supreme are somehow separate and exclusive of one another. I prefer the Taoist pointer of the man of understanding as being a perfectly ordinary human. He eats when he is hungry, he works to provide for himself and his family, he takes pleasure in his sexuality and cries when he hurts. He lives in accord with his nature.

One of my favorite remembrances of Ramesh is of him yelling passionately at the television during an episode of Who Wants To Be A Millionaire in which the contestant chose to risk a small fortune to get to the next level... "You bloody fool!!" Ramesh, always the conservative banker, shouted out.

Ramesh was one of the most ordinary of extraordinary men. His life was a testament to this. It was not surprising therefore that he would raise the ire of the modern religious fundamentalists for whom Understanding is synonymous with renunciation and who have very strong ideas about how other people "should" be. Ramesh weathered these often vicious and virulent attacks with typical poise and good humor. "Brickbats and bouquets," he was fond of saying. I admit I didn't know what a brickbat was (it's a club) but I got his point that in this life some people throw you love (bouquets) and others throw you hate (brickbats) and ultimately what they are throwing is more about them than it is about you.

With much love,

Wayne

Hello my loves,

Niels Bohr, the famous physicist said. "It is wrong to think that the task of physics is to find out how nature IS. Physics concerns what we SAY about nature." I think this statement applies equally well to spirituality and religion. All discussions about God, Source or Enlightenment are discussions about what has been SAID on the subject, even if it was said by your own mind.

The mind confuses its ability to label and compare things with actually knowing what something IS. This fundamental misunderstanding is at the root of human discontent. It is not the limitation itself that causes the discontent, it is the ignorance about the limitation. Most people believe that what they think to be true is True in the Absolute sense, rather than realizing that it is true in only the limited relative sense.

This is why the Living Teaching focuses on your essential nature, encouraging you too follow your curiosity as it pertains to What You Are rather than what you imagine yourself to be.

There are many paths to the edge of the cliff. The one you are on can be glimpsed by looking back over your shoulder.

With much love,

Wayne

Hello my loves,

The end of the year is a natural time to stop and reflect.
Dredge the memory. Wonder about the future.

For me the year embodied the reality of polaric opposites.
My beloved guru, Ramesh and his dear wife, Sharda both
died. Their passing was intensely painful. Their absence
left a hole of galactic dimension. As I watched the DVD of
Ramesh's last Talk I was overwhelmed with gratitude for
having known this great man. He was frail and weak and
in a sense, barely there, yet he was still talking and teaching
and leading his visitor into a deeper insight into the Reality
that was palpable in the room. His presence spoke volumes
more than his words. That which is born must die. That
which was never born is eternal.

With great sadness comes great joy. My first grandchild,
Hailey was born and I was able to hold her within a few
minutes of her birth and experience that exquisite connection
that is the essence of our humanity. Watching her grow and
develop, smile, laugh, recognize and grasp is one of life's
spectacular gifts.

As has been the case for so many years now, I
traveled the world and sat intimately with many people.
Overcoming the barriers of language and custom through
meeting with open hearts and open minds. I feel blessed
to be able to participate in the sharing of this legacy left
by my beloved Ramesh...though sometimes when I hear
myself say something particularly outlandish I have

an immediate vision of Ramesh shaking his head and tolerantly smiling at me (a look I had numerous occasions to see).

This is a Living Teaching we are engaged in. It pulses and throbs with life in all its vital aspects. It caresses us and stabs us and all the while it IS us. What a crazy miracle! I hope you can join me in celebrating it NOW!

With much love,

Wayne

Hello My Loves,

People often point to human pain and misery and ask why it exists. This Living Teaching offers no simple answers. The key word there is simple. The structure of the Universe, of which humans are but a minute part, is infinitely vast and complex. The human brain simply isn't equipped with sufficient processing power to see all the links and relationships of the Universe. Therefore any answer to WHY things happen is incomplete, simplistic (no matter how complicated) and ultimately arbitrary.

When faced with images of human pain and misery as with the recent earthquake in Haiti, many of us are moved and touched. We empathize, which is to say that we feel within ourselves some of the pain of others. It is an aspect of our humanness. Only the most spiritually naive dismiss it as unreal, an apparition, a dream. After all, it is as real as you are and it is logically ridiculous to assert your own unreality. Depending on your nature you may be moved to action or you may be moved to seek to understand or more likely to some combination of the two.

It may be worth investigating why it is you want to understand. Isn't it that you are uncomfortable not knowing? When you don't understand there is the discomfort of feeling out of control. If this is so, the understanding that is sought is actually a vehicle to comfort. Comfort being the objective, there are many ways to reach it, at least temporarily. Religious explanations, philosophical explanations and scientifc explanations all may bring a degree of comfort if not examined too deeply.

The Living Teaching is about looking deeply. When engaged in rigorously you WILL be uncomfortable since the Teaching pushes you out of your comfort zone. With Grace you will be pushed out of the nest and into the freefall which is mystical Understanding...conceptless, open and free. It is a space of infinite potential in which you know yourself as BOTH the Limitless and the limited. May it find you now.

With much love,

Wayne

Hello my loves,

The bondage of certainty.

To believe that you know the truth is to live in a prison.

From there there can be no further movement. Perhaps you know that all is One. Perhaps you know you do not exist or that everything is an illusion. All you are convinced you know is true are the shackles that restrict your ability to live freely.

It IS the way of things. But occasionally comes the courage to escape. A crack opens in the cell wall and you dig through it toward the light beyond. It is however a narrow passage and to squeeze through it you must leave everything behind.

To walk naked in a world where most everyone else is clothed takes courage indeed.

May it find you now.

With love,

Wayne

Hello my loves,

    I am not the body.
    I am not the body.
    And yet I AM

    So what is the body?

    An illusion? An annoyance?
    A vehicle for pleasure? A vehicle for pain?
    The fragile vessel for a life lived?

    As I lay in the emergency room, my heart rate dipping
    into the low 30's, I was not afraid to die...
    I did however have plans and desires.
    I wanted to see my daughter and granddaughter, due
    to arrive in two days.
    I wanted to know how my wife, Jaki's new book was
    going to do.
    I wanted to have a few more great meals.
    I wanted to make love some more.
    I wanted to scuba dive again.

    This body was born into an age of technological wizardry.
    The healers came and laid on their skilled hands.
    A device was inserted and connected to my heart.
    I was resurrected.
    My heart beats strong and steady.

Every day of life is a miracle
In which the Oneness moves as the many.

I am not the body
And yet I AM.

With much love,

Wayne

Hello my loves,

Of the many complex and often confusing concepts that arise in this Teaching, perhaps one of the most difficult is the distinction between duality and dualism.

This is made all the more confusing because this Teaching is often called Nonduality when it should more rightly be called Nondualism.

Dualism is by its very nature judgmental and exclusive. It suggests that there is no Unity now. Unity is imagined as the future perfect state in which what is presently considered to be bad, evil and painful is eliminated. Dualism is thus linked to suffering because in dualism, What Is manifest now — and this of course includes you — is thought to be incomplete, flawed and in desperate need of revision. In dualism, duality is seen as a flaw to be overcome. In dualism, Enlightenment is viewed as the end of duality.

The term duality is descriptive. It points to the experiential fact that the Whole is made manifest through the harmony of polaric opposites. The yin/yang symbol visually expresses this principle. Duality is a term that affirms What Is. It INCLUDES the negative, painful and unpleasant and acknowledges that they exist as part of the Unity. Duality can thus be considered to be the structure of the phenomenal world which is understood to be a manifestation of the

Source. Implicit in duality is acceptance of What IS — which of course includes you. In duality, Enlightenment is viewed as the end of dualism.

I hope this helps.

With love,

Wayne

Hello my loves,

Today (May 25) is Ramesh's birthday. Normally, I would call him and wish him a Happy Birthday and inquire about his health and if the monsoon had come yet and how many intrepid seekers were braving the heat/wet to come to the morning Talks. He would tell me about his latest book and perhaps ask me what I thought of this title or that. I would hear about the latest precocious comment from his great-grandson and about the latest goings and comings of the extended family that lives in the building. We would never talk for very long, neither one of us being all that fond of chit chat, but the connection was made. Our bodies warmed by the sound of the voice of the other. Such a little thing, really, in the overall scheme of things but such an integral part of my life for over twenty years. I miss not being able to call him today. It makes me a little sad. The sadness is the flip side of the joy I have in knowing him. Two sides of the same coin that enriches me.

I am very grateful. People often express surprise when I say that...as if it is an unAdvaita thing to say...but this life is amazing! That it is possible to laugh and cry and feel pleasure and pain...to gaze into a sky that is so blue that it hurts and watch a hawk circle upwards in a thermal while my nine month old granddaughter coos happily against my chest...what a gift!

May your days be free from the bondage of philosophy (even the philosophy of non-duality) so that your heart can soar and your spirit dance even when you are sad and miss someone you love.

With much love,

Wayne

Hello my loves,

Our minds want to know the 'how?' and 'why?' of things. This natural drive to know is very useful when it comes to functioning in the world. It helps us organize the vast amount of information our senses deliver to our brains. However when it comes to the task of apperceiving the Truth we must shift our gaze to the 'what' of things.

The Living Teaching directs your attention to What Is in this moment. The Seeing it encourages is preintellectual. It is the delicate kiss of child-like curiosity applied to all that the senses touch...and beyond.

The process is happening to you and through You. Relax and enjoy when you can.

With much love

Hello my loves,

"How will I know when I see it?"
"How do I look?"
These are the questions that inevitably follow when I say, "look deeply. See what lies beyond the surface."
There is no "how" to looking. It is like breathing. It happens. Sure you can train yourself to modify your breathing but the breathing itself requires no effort or skill. Like your breathing, this looking is happening all the time. What the Teaching may bring is awareness of What Is... here, now in this eternal moment. To see it, only looking is necessary.
The question of "how do I do this looking?" is usually tied to the persistent involvement by the False Sense of Authorship. The FSA's job is to claim that it is responsible for what you do, therefore when you contemplate doing something there is inevitably an overlay of tension and fear. "What if I fail? What if I do it wrong?" When the FSA is active and claiming to be the "I" that does things, there can be no peace.
Look deeply without a "how."
How?
Just do it!!

Much love,
Wayne

Hello my loves,

Ramesh used to talk about what he called non volitional living. Simply put, non volitional living means to act without a claim of authorship for your actions. He was fond of pointing out that to live non volitionally means to live harmoniously with What Is, but he was quick to add that to volitionally decide to live non volitionally was not likely to yield the desired result.

Non volitional living is the recognition of the true state of things. It is to see that getting angry is a result of the same forces as the changing of the seasons or the transformation of a bud into a flower. It is seeing that what we are is the same as what everything else is. It is the recognition that all is an inseparable Whole.

Totally simple. Totally obvious...once you glimpse. Then you are changed forever.

Much love,

Wayne

Hello my loves,

September is a meaningful month for me. It was in September of 1987 that Ramesh Balsekar entered my life and it was September 2009 when his physical presence left my life. It is impossible to explain to someone who has not experienced the guru/disciple relationship what such a relationship means. It is easily ridiculed or minimized by those who have not known it.

I am reminded of the phrase: Those who hear not the music, think the dancer is mad!

It is one of the greatest blessings of my life to have heard the music and danced that sacred dance with Ramesh. Whether others understand or not is of no consequence. Twenty three years ago I fell in love with a diminutive Indian banker and my life changed irrevocably. Even though his body is no more, he continues to live inside me as a powerful presence. I think of him often and honor his inspiration and guidance in every Talk I am asked to give.

Ramesh was the most generous person I ever met. He gave unceasingly of his time and his energy to all who came to him. Even on his deathbed he remained available to those whose devotion pulled them to be near him. He was a great man, a brilliant teacher and my guru.

On this, the first anniversary of his death, I celebrate the gift that he was and continues to be. Through his books and recordings he will continue to help dispel the darkness for countless people who will never meet him in the flesh. For those of us graced with the opportunity to sit at his feet, he will live on in our hearts forever.

With much love,

Wayne

Hello my loves,

Two books have appeared this month in the Advaita Press store and I must say that I am delighted with both of them.

The first is a reprint of the long out of print book, "From Consciousness To Consciousness" by Ramesh. It delights me because it was the second of Ramesh's books that I published and it reminds me of the truism, "everyone gets to wear the clown suit." The year was 1988 and it was my (and my dear friend Rifka's) first attempt to organize Ramesh's tour in the States. Ramesh had just received the manuscript of the book from Ben and was very anxious to have it available for the tour. There was not time to bring out a perfect-bound book so I decided to publish it as a staple-spined booklet. After much frantic rushing around, the booklet was printed and picked up at the printer on the night before Ramesh arrived in LA. The following day we began our drive up the coast. During the Talks in Tiburon, someone came up to me waving the booklet entitled "From Conciousness To Conciousness" and saying, "shouldn't "conciousness" have another 's' in it?" My heart sank with a thud. I had misspelled the word "consciousness" right there on the cover (where no one would notice)!!! The book has now been reprinted with "consciousness" spelled properly and the content as lively and as relevant today as it was 20+ years ago.

The other book is "Calm Is Greater Than Joy" edited by Shirish Murthy (arguably Ramesh's most dedicated devotee). Those of you who visited Ramesh in Bombay will remember "Murthy" as the soft-spoken, kind and helpful presence who guided people to the "hot seat" in front of Ramesh. His book is a fascinating comparison of the Teachings of Ramana Maharshi, Nisargadatta Maharaj, Ramesh Balsekar and me. He selected many different topics and then presented comments from each of the four of us relating to each topic. It is a very fine book; quite obviously a labor of love from someone with a deep understanding of the Teaching.

With much love

Wayne

Hello my loves,

Today finds me more cranky and belligerent than usual. Perhaps it is jet lag, perhaps it's the weather or maybe it's just my deepest self emerging...whatever the case I am moved to write about the latest nondual fad of "I don't exist." It seems I am hearing it more and more as people who realize they don't exist are told by others that this means they are enlightened and set up shop helping others to realize that they too don't exist. It is inevitable, I suppose, (every pointer to the Truth turns toxic eventually) but it makes my job that much harder and despite my role as Total Love and Ultimate Acceptance I find it irritating as hell.

I used the same pointer for many years, myself. I would often say, "No one in the entire history of mankind has ever been enlightened and you are not going to be the first." Or "Enlightenment is seeing that there is no one to be enlightened." Such statements were meant to provoke a deeper investigation into the nature of who you consider yourself to be....they were never intended to be taken literally. But the mind is always seeking something solid it can grasp and know...even if it is a negative something such as "you don't exist."

Ramesh used to say that the sage was the maha-boghi, the supreme enjoyer or supreme experiencer. This was in direct contrast to the widely held notion that enlightenment brought an empty sameness, in which everything was seen as an illusion or a dull, greyness in which everything was known to be the same.

The sense of self, such that you know yourself as distinct from the armchair, is a functional reality. What happens in humans is that at the age of roughly 2 1/2, this sense of self gets hijacked by a false sense of self-as-the-author (FSA). The FSA is like ivy that grows up a tree and finally covers it to the point that you can't imagine the tree without the ivy. To get rid of the ivy you conclude you must chop down the tree. But if you chop down the tree what is left to experience? However, if you get rid of the ivy you are left with a beautiful, healthy tree to enjoy. The sense of self without its covering of parasitic FSA is truly a thing of beauty. It is the vehicle for life, love, happiness, sadness, pain, misery, joy and wonder. All experience is connected to an experiencer and that is the Self expressing itself as you.

With much love,

Wayne

Hello my loves,

The end of the year is often a time of reflection and evaluation, a time to take stock of things. When doing so it is good to remember that life is composed of polaric opposites...good and bad, pleasure and pain, joy and sorrow. Too often there is a sense that things shouldn't be the way they are...particularly the unpleasant and painful aspects of life. It is an area ripe for intrusion by the FSA (false sense of authorship)...which is the claim that you should have done it better and IF you had done it better then life would have been better.

The antidote to the suffering that comes with the sense that you are responsible for life's ills (if not all of them at least some of them) is simple awareness. We are blessed with this wonderful Teaching that often stimulates such awareness. The Teaching is so clear and elemental. It is like water. You can see through it yet, like water it supports you and carries you along. It is also like air in that though you can't see it it sustains you. In such clarity there is no impediment to seeing that which lies beyond. It is a great gift.

When looking back at the year, don't forget to include it on the positive side of the ledger.

I wish you all peace amidst the vibrant ecstasy and exquisite agony that Life contains.

With much love,

Wayne

Hello My Loves,

Many thanks to all of you who helped me celebrate 60 years of life! It was a wonderful party and I was quite moved by the outpouring of love and devotion so many of you expressed. Of the many gifts given me in this life I count chief among them the gift of having met Ramesh and being graced with this amazing Teaching. That I am today able to share this gift with others fills me with wonder and gratitude. That others find what I do valuable pleases me greatly.

As you know, I am the most unlikely of teachers. Neither my history as an alcoholic and drug addicted businessman nor my introverted (some would say asocial) temperament fit the image of what a spiritual teacher looks like. It is clear to me that I live the way I live today and do the things I do today not because of any plan or aspiration on my part but because the Universe has unfolded in this particular way.

Humility and gratitude are not things to accomplish; they are the natural and inevitable consequence of seeing What Is, here and now, in this eternal moment. How this seeing comes about is the essence of the Eternal Mystery that surrounds us.

With much love,

Wayne

Hello my loves,

Spring comes
And the grass
Grows by itself

I love this exquisite haiku. It captures the subtlety and simplicity of this Living Teaching. The coming of spring is a happening. The growing of the grass is a happening. The human brain links these happenings in a simplistic (not simple) relationship of cause and effect. The simple (not simplistic) understanding is that these two happenings are aspects of an unbroken Wholeness, inseparable from each other and from everything else.

The ever practical brain wants to know what earthly good is such esoteric understanding? How does it help us grow more and better grass? How does it feed us? How can it enrich us? The answer is that it is of no practical value. It does not help us to manage life better.

But its mystical value is immeasurable. It enables us to be at peace even when our minds and bodies are in turmoil... not as an act of skill, not as an achievement but as an act of Grace.

May it find you now!

With love

Wayne

Hello my loves,

Advaita often gets a bad rap when it comes to the subject of morality. It is mistakenly assumed that if everything is understood to be One then good and bad, right and wrong don't exist. In the Living Teaching of Advaita, morality is seen to be an integral part of the human experience. In this moment all of us have a set of values that is linked to our behavior. For example, we likely feel it is wrong to be unkind to those that we love. To hurt someone we love would violate our moral code. Yet most of us from time to time find ourselves doing just that. We hurt the ones we love with anger or neglect even though we know it to be wrong. Why do we do it? How is it that we act in opposition to our own moral code? Could it be that we are powerless to control our own behavior at least some of the time? If so, then what IS controlling our behavior? It may be worth investigating...

Morality is simply the evaluation of behavior according to a standard. The much deeper and revealing question deals with the Source of behavior. Once we begin to understand what is the true Source of all that we think and do and feel the ensuing moralistic evaluation loses its cruel energy. It is still there as part of our human makeup but it no longer causes us to suffer. We do not claim authorship of our actions but we are not sociopaths. Our morality signals an opportunity to try to right any wrongs we have done without the enervating sense of guilt and shame. We can look the world in the eye, admit we were wrong, clean up any mess we may have made and then get on with our lives. What a blessing!

May it find you now.

With much love,

Wayne

Hello my loves,

One of my favorite things in life is to watch the Teaching take root in someone and begin to grow. It is the excitement of Spring. Blossoming and unfolding.

The most fun is when the person isn't already a spiritual seeker, but someone that the Universe has simply dragged out of their familiar life and thrust into the bizarre world of one of my Talks. They come not knowing what to expect, usually a little hesitant and confused by the new language and strangely charged atmosphere. They listen for a while and then their brow furrows and a question rises to the surface like a bubble long trapped underwater.

"Do you really mean that?" they ask.

"I do. But you need to look and see it for yourself."

I can see it on their face, the insight unfurling like a plant from a seed in a time lapse movie, straining towards the light. Suddenly it breaks free and there is a rush of activity as all the implications branch out. Well then that would mean.....and that would mean.....and what about personal responsibility?

It is literally mind blowing. All the assumptions about who and what they are come crashing down. How will I live? What do I do now?

This Living Teaching is capable of inciting enormous changes. Once the truth of What Is is glimpsed, there is no going back to full ignorance. The progression may be fast or slow but it is inexorable.

As Ram Tzu says,

Once the Teaching takes hold
You have a cancer
It will gradually replace you with Itself
Until you are gone.

With love,

Wayne

Hello my loves,

Personal power is the belief that 'I' have the power to make things happen. It is the sense that 'I' control myself and my environment. It stems from the observation that the more power you have, the more control you can exert. The difficulty with this premise is that it continuously proves to be false. The fact is that the power is never yours. It flows through you and controls you. Deep investigation may even reveal that this power not only flows through you and controls you but it IS you.

One of the surprising gifts of the Living Teaching is to discover your own personal powerlessness. Personal powerlessness may not seem like a gift on the surface, in fact if you google the term 'powerlessness' you will quickly see that the world-at-large considers powerlessness to be a condition requiring treatment. It is another of the paradoxes of the Teaching that personal strength can be found in the realization of your own personal powerlessness. Ironically, this personal strength comes from the relief of the burden of trying to exert power and control that was never yours to begin with. Suddenly you may find yourself with all the extra energy that was formerly being poured into the fruitless attempt to make things go your way.

As with all aspects of the Living Teaching, what I am pointing to has to be seen to be believed. Consider what I am saying and test it for yourself. Look within to discover the Truth that is as close to you as your breath.

May it find you now.

With love,

Wayne

Hello my loves,

If you were fortunate enough to have visited Ramesh
in Mumbai then you will likely have had the pleasure to
meet his brother Chaitan. Chaitan shared Ramesh's lifelong
interest in Advaita and the two would often visit the Talks
of Nisargadatta Maharaj together. I recently received a new
book entitled "Dream of Consciousness" written by Chaitan
and was delighted by its simplicity and clarity. It is truly
a lovely book. It presents the often difficult Teachings of
Ramana, Nisargadatta and Ramesh in a light and accessible
way. I recommend it highly.

I am about to depart on my favorite trip of the year. This
weekend I will visit with old friends and new in the lovely
city of Barcelona before heading east to Moscow and Kiev.
I am blessed beyond measure to have the opportunity to
share this magnificent Teaching with so many wonderful
people.

The trip culminates with a week long gathering on the
island of Ibiza during which we meet daily for Talks, a swim
and a superb lunch. It is a great pleasure for me to spend a
week with the same group of people and watch the Silence
grow and the Seeing deepen.

The beauty of the Living Teaching is that it embraces
the entirety of life and living. It is not afraid of pleasure
nor does it make a virtue of austerity and renunciation. All

is understood to be a manifestation of the Life Source. So enjoy if you can and suffer if you must but realize that ALL is playing out in perfect harmony.

With love,

Wayne

Hello my loves,

I think it bears repeating that the Living Teaching is about living. Sometimes in the thrill and excitement of chasing Ultimate Understanding or Silent, Still Spaciousness it is possible to lose sight of the miracles that abound all around us. Quite simply, life is amazing! But please don't take my word for this or ask me to elaborate on which things are so fantastic. Far better that you look for yourself. With Grace these words will trigger something in you. Perhaps you will pause from reading this long enough to take a look around you or in you. Perhaps you will catch a glimpse of the underlying Unity of all things that is made manifest in all that exists. What could be more miraculous?

I can think of nothing more wondrous than walking the earth comfortable inside your own skin. This Gift accompanies the direct seeing of who and what you truly are.

May it find you now!

With love,

Wayne

Hello my loves,

Where I often see people getting stuck in the Teaching is in the relationship between the Absolute and the relative. Obviously in daily life we have the relative, the dualistic in which there are polaric opposites...me and you, truth and falsehood, sickness and heath, good and bad. Yet what all the spiritual teachings are pointing at is Oneness beyond the dualistic. How often have you heard, "I am not somebody, I am That!" When taken from an imagined non-dual perspective the inevitable question is, "How can there be relativity if its all One?"

That there can experientally be the appearance of the many without destroying the Wholeness is the incredible, beautiful paradox that is implicit in being alive.

Within dualistic experience there is the appearance of separation, an appearance of this and that even though inherently it is all One. Oneness can best be understood as the container for the dualistic. The polaric opposites are the building blocks that make up manifest life. That is why I like the image of the Ocean (Source, God, Stillness, Oneness) and the waves (you, me, stars, quarks) so much. Within this image both exist simultaneously. There are billions of unique waves and yet all a wave is, is Ocean. A wave is nothing more and nothing less than an energetic movement of Ocean. Despite its appearance, a wave isn't a moving packet of water. What we call a wave is simply a movement of energy through the Ocean. It doesn't have any identifiable substance other than as a momentary shape of Ocean. So does a wave actually exist?

I think Ramana Maharshi answered it best, "It is as real as You are."

With love,

Wayne

Hello my loves,

It has been two years now since Ramesh left this realm. I think of him often. His spirit infuses me like the air I breathe. Apart and of me at the same time. Thinking of him makes me smile. Sometimes its a sad smile as I realize that I can't pick up the phone and talk to him...not that either one of us were sparkling conversationalists on the phone...but the sound of his voice and knowing that he was sitting in his chair in his bedroom brought me comfort and pleasure. Usually when I think of him it is with a smile of wonder and delight as I feel his presence within me.

But what I feel most often is Gratitude. I am so grateful for the gift that Ramesh is in my life. To meet and know one's Guru is the greatest of miracles. For me it has been twenty-four years and ten days since our first meeting. My biggest smile is reserved for the memory of that day and the recognition that walking into that room I had no clue that my life was about to be radically transformed in ways I couldn't possibly imagine. Such is the exquisite beauty of life and living...like licking honey off a thorn.

I know many of you reading this were also deeply affected by Ramesh and his Teaching. I am sure you will join me today in celebrating the life of this extraordinary Being.

With love,

Wayne

Hello my loves,

Years ago there was a very popular self-help book entitled "Women Who Love Too Much". I never read the book but the title continues to haunt me. Is it actually possible to love too much? I think not. It is certainly possible to expect too much. It is possible to enter into a transactional relationship and get the short end of the deal. It is possible to be cheated and disappointed when the other person fails to deliver their end of the bargain. But that is not my vision of Love.

Love to me is totally selfless and nontransactional. Love like this is known in the giving rather than the getting. Giving everything.

Including your self.

It is impossible to give too much in such a relationship. It is impossible to be cheated when you expect nothing in return. To receive such Love is to be totally accepted as you are.

To give such love is to know Peace.

With love,

Wayne

Hello my loves,

Our only obligation in life is to live it. The word obligation within the Living Teaching simply means we have to do it. We have no choice in the matter. We must live because we are the life force itself, incarnated as a particular name and form.

The most common question that arises with this is, "how do I live my life knowing I am not the author of my thoughts, feelings and actions?"

The fact that the question arises indicates that the comprehension of "I am not the author" is at the intellectual level. A good start certainly, but an indicator that there is a deepening yet to come.

As the understanding deepens there comes the intuitive recognition that we are being lived. Then the question of "how do I live" fades into the mist. It is not replaced with an answer. It is simply gone.

Spontaneous living is always happening but it is only experienced as such in the absence of the false sense of authorship (FSA). When the FSA is present it brings with it the weighty burden of personal responsibility. Personal responsibility is a much glorified concept that everyone knows from their own experience can only sporadically be observed. Still it persists as an exalted goal. The notion of personal responsibility is the most common obstacle to intellectual acceptance of the Living

Teaching. It is the stronghold of the FSA. Yet as we are privileged to witness again and again, cracks can and do form in the foundations of the most formidable citadels. As the cracks widen and spread they can bring down the entire structure and when the dust settles te simple Truth is revealed.

May it find you now.

With love,

Wayne

Hello my loves,

If you open your eyes and look around, you can't help but marvel. Life in all its amazing diversity there to behold. Like the woman who used to sit on the sidewalk at the corner of Ramesh's block in Bombay selling bananas. Amidst the filth and billowing clouds of exhaust she sat, immaculately groomed and seemingly serene, her round basket of bananas set out before her.

See the patterns the shadows make on the wall? Listen to the sound of the small plane overhead. Someone is up there looking down on where you are and to them it is but a speck, if they notice at all. A bird jumps from the fence to the ground to eat a worm and another bird darts in to steal the meal. Which one eats it is probably of little consequence to the worm, and I certainly have no preference, but the birds seem to care. The wind comes up and the bamboo clacks together in primal music. My stomach rumbles. Somewhere someone has just won the lottery and their financial problems are over, soon to be replaced with a whole new set of problems. My excited daughter calls to tell me she is pregnant again. An email comes announcing the funeral for an old friend. A pretty girl passes and my gaze follows her. Close your eyes and watch the show that plays out on the inside of your eyelids. Smell your fingers and remember where they have been.

Anywhere your attention moves there is something to be discovered. You need only lift your gaze from the demands of your 'self' to realize the miracle that is life and living.

May it find you now.

With love,

Wayne

Hello my loves,

So I had a choice this morning. To sit down and write a short piece that Rebecca needs so she can get the January newsletter out before the end of the month (and that might even help some people) OR I could follow a link on lifehacker.com to add homemade noise cancelling foam pads to my ear buds for my iPod (which I really don't need and which would require a trip to the hardware store to get a hole punch). So what did I do?

Wow, you should see these ear buds, they're really cool! And quiet!!

This raises the question, "What makes us act in ways that are opposite to what we believe to be best?" If we truly had the power to control our actions, wouldn't we always do what we thought was best? Would we ever shirk our responsibilities or act in ways that ran counter to our own values?

This is a question you must answer for yourself. And it won't work to simply say, "Yes, but I am lazy." That may be true but it avoids the deeper recognition of the fact that you lack the power to always control your laziness. You may be lazy but did you make yourself lazy? Or are you powerless over your own laziness?

If you are very blessed you may be a person with a lot of what we call "self-discipline." This means that your actions most often match your feeling of what you "should" do. However, the sameessential question applies. Did you create your character or was it shaped by countless forces beyond your control?

To come face to face with your own ultimate powerlessness is the key to discovering what Ramesh called, "Peace and Harmony In Daily Living."

May it find you now.

With love,

Wayne

Hello my loves,

The guru is the dispeller of illusions. The primary illusion is that of being a separate, independent, powerful entity. But there are many secondary illusions as well. For long time followers of Advaita the most powerful illusion is that of believing you are Source. This belief is particularly seductive when it masquerades as deep knowing. Here is where the guru is of greatest value. Unconcerned about matters of doctrine or personal popularity, the guru can see the seekers obstruction and point the way to clarity (even if the seeker no longer considers himself a seeker).

Unfortunately the ego (FSA) often puts up an agonizing fight at this point. It has fallen back to its final defensive position of claiming to know the Truth. As sometimes happens, the seeker may even be in the embarrassing position of being a spiritual teacher. Whether teacher or advanced student, and regardless of life circumstance Grace happens. The illusion is dispelled. That which has always been is revealed. Profoundly simple. Wondrously ordinary. Here. Now. Eternal.

With love,

Wayne

Hello my loves,

I am often asked for advice and I never give it. I prefer to give love, support and acceptance for whatever it is you end up doing. Even if I dislike your action, I am clear that my reaction is about me not you. There is no doubt whatsoever that whatever you do is the product of vast Universal forces and could no more be otherwise than the moon could be in some other position than it is in this moment. The same acceptance washes over my own reaction to what you do. There is not the slightest stirring of a story about how my reaction could have been or should have been otherwise. All is unfolding absolutely perfectly. Could it get more simple?

May such Realization find you now.

With much love,

Wayne

Hello my loves,

The ecstatic state of Now is one of life's supreme joys. The critical thing to remember about the ecstatic state of Now is that it comes and it goes. Furthermore, there is nothing you can do that will reliably produce it and there is nothing you can do to reliably keep it. The good news in all this is that when it goes it does not go because of something you have done or haven't done. You do not have the inherent power to screw it up!

So if there is nothing you can do (as an author) to make it happen or to keep it from happening, where does that leave you? The answer of course is quite simple:

It leaves you here, Now!

With much love,

Hello my loves,

To be relieved of the bondage of self is to realize that the self that claims responsibility for things is a phantom, it does not exist except in our unconscious imaginations. When this is first grasped it is tempting to throw out the entire idea of being a self and begin to identify exclusively as Source but with time and maturity this proves to be unnecessary.

When we look into the question of self ever more deeply we come to realize that what keeps us in bondage is not the self, per se, but the false sense of authorship that has hijacked the self and subverted it. It is a subtle but crucial distinction we make here but looking into it can save you a lot of awkwardness and grief. I can't tell you how many people over the years have come to me and proudly proclaimed that they are nobody!

Nisargadatta Maharaj said it beautifully. "When you understand the meaning of "Self" there will be no room for selfishness. Understand this thoroughly, abide in it, then in due course you will realize it. When the time is ripe, then it will happen."

May it find you now!

With much love,

Wayne

Hello my loves,

Lets face it. We are driven by the demands of food, sex and territory. Anyone who has ever found themselves in silent battle for a few millimeters of space on the armrest of a crowded plane, anyone who has risked family and reputation for an illicit sexual adventure, anyone who has left the comfort of a warm bed to go to work knows the power of these demands. They exist in a place beyond logic, reason and good sense. They are primal and relentless. In the face of such demands we are stripped to our basic natures. It is a wonder that we are able to keep up the pretense that we are in control and the masters of our destinies. Yet that is precisely the role of the False Sense of Authorship. It is the master of pretense and nothing else. When we glimpse this, the door to freedom cracks open.

May it find you now.

With much love,

Wayne

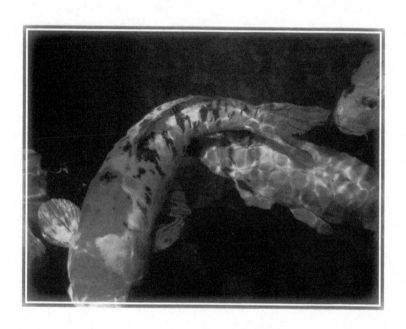

Hello my loves...

I am very excited to tell you about a project that I have been working on for the last several years. It is a book entitled *The Way of Powerlessness -- Advaita and the Twelve Steps of Recovery*. What makes it significant for me is that it is the first book since No Way in 1989 that I have built from the ground up. My previous three books all began as transcripts of Talks which we subsequently edited and embellished. The writing process has always been excruciatingly slow and erratic for me, but in this case, I finally have been empowered to finish it. What's more, the result I think is good. It brings together two themes that have run parallel in my life for over twenty-five years.

For those of you unfamiliar with the Twelve Steps of Alcoholics Anonymous, the book may be a surprise. In it you can discover a series of Steps that have helped millions of people find a way of life based on recognizing their powerlessness and becoming free of the bondage of "self" (what we call the False Sense of Authorship). For those who are graced with the ability to complete the Steps, the results are nearly always positive, and often are quite spectacular. You might also be surprised to see how these principles, that are so prominent in Advaita, are mirrored in the Twelve Steps of recovery.

Inshallah, the publication date is September 1, 2012. As always, we will see what happens! We will send you a notice as soon as the books arrive. I hope you like it!

With much love,

Wayne

Hello my loves...

This month marks exactly 25 years since I first met Ramesh and my life changed beyond my wildest imaginings. It also sees the publication of a book, The Way of Powerlessness - Advaita and the 12 Steps of Recovery, that has brought together some of the bounty I received from Ramesh as well as some of the incredible wisdom embodied in the 12 Steps of Alcoholics Anonymous.

Ramesh's eldest son became addicted to alcohol in the latter stage of his life and finally succumbed to a variety of health issues. Some years after his death I shared with Ramesh some of my thoughts about my own alcoholism and how it led me to the 12 Steps and ultimately to him. With moist eyes he looked directly at me and quietly said, "Alcohol took one of my sons, but gave me another."

I am filled with gratitude for all that this life has given me. The pleasure and the pain. The joy and the sorrow. Ramesh and the 12 Steps. I feel blessed to be able to share some of this with you and others.

Sending a book out into the world is a bit like sending your child off to college. What happens next is out of your view -- though every once in a while there is a call home. I look forward to the occasional report about how the book is doing, but after so many years of living with it, I am glad to see it go. I wish it well.

There is incredible Peace to be had in life. It is here, touching everything. The Living Teaching of Advaita and the 12 Steps are both potent pointers to this Peace.

May it find you now.

With love,

Wayne

Hello my loves,

I have a great many blessings in my life. I won't try to list them as there are far too many, but certainly at the top of the list would be Kind, Loving People. I get to meet a lot of such people. Some come into my life through the front door of my home which is opened four days a week for Talks. Others I meet through the Talks I give when I travel. Still more write to me or send me emails. Some are in prison, some in remote towns or villages where Advaita is as unimaginable as snow in Samoa. It is a joy to have such rich connections with people.

The flip side to all this pleasure is the pain of losing someone with whom I have formed a heart connection. This weekend came the pain of losing Cat Asche and Chris Bava who were killed in a traffic accident. My life and Cat and Chris's lives entwined for more than a decade. Cat edited my book Acceptance of What IS and was amazingly generous at a time when I was in need. Chris shared Cat's kind and generous heart. He was a man who had wrestled with many demons and he had emerged to share his strength and his hope with others caught in the same battle. I loved them both.

Life contains birth and death. It is the way of things. Humans experience joy and sorrow. It is the way of things. What happened, happened -- there is no going back -- there is no "might have been." The bodies of Cat and Chris are gone and I am very sad but the energy of who they were and how they lived continues in our memories and in the lives of all they touched. There is freedom in the simple recognition of this.

May it find you now!

With love,

Wayne

Hello my loves,

I'd like to talk a bit about Gratitude.

In America we have just finished our Thanksgiving holiday which is traditionally an occasion to watch American football on TV, overeat and perhaps to take a moment to look around and see if there is anything to be thankful for. This latter is where it gets interesting. Some people have no difficulty rattling off a long string of things that they are grateful for. Others can barely come up with one. As far as they are concerned the world is going to hell. Economic disaster is just around the corner. The ice cap is melting. Cancer is everywhere. Violence is in the air.

What is responsible for such a difference?

It would be easy to dismiss the question with the simple observation that some people are optimists and others pessimists but it really goes much deeper than that. On the surface it is plain to see that there are events we consider good and others we consider bad. When our attention is focused on the good we are happy and optimistic, when focused on the bad we are sad and pessimistic. Optimists tell pessimists to quit being so negative and to focus on all the joy and beauty that abounds. Pessimists tell optimists to quit being so airy-fairy and to recognize that there are enormous problems threatening our very existence.

Gratitude within the context of the Living Teaching transcends such limited, polaric attitudes. We recognize that life is by its very nature rich and complex. It has always contained within it the seeds for annihilation and resurrection. We cannot possibly predict what the future will hold. In the Living Teaching we abide in the wisdom of BOTH. The positive and negative are recognized as the essential building blocks of the manifest world. We are grateful for the lack of limitation which makes anything possible and live comfortably in the vastness of the present moment.

May it find you now!

With love,

Wayne

Hello my loves,

Life is a dance. We are dancing...we are being danced... we twirl and spin and leap and exalt in the sheer joy of this dance. There are no wallflowers here. It is all dance floor. It matters not if we have a partner dancing opposite us. We are joined in the dance by all the other dancers. We are all in this ballroom together, bound by the music and compelled to move to its rhythm.

No it is not always graceful. We bump into each other, trip over feet...others and our own. Sometimes we fall.

Funny thing about this dance of ours...the harder we try the more clumsy we become. Our grace is in the letting go. When we surrender to the music it is free to move through us unrestricted. Our bodies and minds sway freely, smooth and effortless. It is ecstasy, in its purest, simplest and most mundane form.

We are blessed indeed to hear the divine choruses, even though those who hear not the music, think we dancers are mad!

May your dance be joyous and effortless in the coming year!

With much love,

Wayne

Hello my loves,

Life is so simple. No, really, I mean it! There are endless things for you to do and all you need do is do them. Starting with breathing....you need to breathe...don't forget that part! But wait...often you forget about breathing altogether and yet you continue to breathe anyway. Curious. And then there is planning. You need to plan. Planning is important. Everyone says so. But sometimes you get so busy executing a previous plan that you forget to plan the next thing. Then what? Stuff keeps happening anyway. Sometimes you like what happens and sometimes you don't...just like the outcome of your plans.

Most important of all you must make decisions. Endless decisions. Get up or stay in bed? Go to work or the beach? Eat or fast? Exercise or lay around? Chocolate or vanilla? Save the world or read a book? You may even decide to stop making decisions. What happens then? I hate to give away the plot but in the end decisions keep getting made anyway.

Perhaps you are starting to notice a pattern is emerging here. I hope so. Because when you recognize that life is happening, the simplicity becomes obvious and there is peace. May it find you now.

With much love,

Wayne

Hello my loves,

That which is born, dies.

This is the first pointer of the Living Teaching. If you were born you're going to die. Today, tomorrow, a year, ten years, fifty, a hundred...you're going to cease to exist in form and substance. This brings most people down, but sometimes you have to be brought down before you can be brought up. The thing about recognizing that you're going to die is that when the inevitability of this really sinks in you start to truly live...as in fully, completely knowing that THIS right here is It...not in a lame, philosophical way but deeply and intuitively. There is the recognition that all we will ever have is what we have in this moment. The future may or may not come and even if it does come it probably won't look the way we have imagined it.

Anyone who has had a near-death experience, knows this. Be it an accident or an illness or extreme duress if it doesn't kill you it leaves you intensely alive...feeling every molecule of air on your skin, alert to how light bounces off leaves, grateful for perfume and stench, in love with friend and foe alike.

To live with the reality of death need not be a morbid, depressing exercise. If you are able to penetrate the initial fear and go to the very heart of death you may discover a freedom unimaginable.

May it find you now.

With love,

Wayne

Hello my loves,

Have I told you today that I love you? Well, I do.

This may seem strange coming from a nonduality/ Advaita guru. Particularly if you associate nonduality/ Advaita with the idea that you don't exist (a state in which love is problematic, at best). If you are convinced that you are nobody please feel free to stop reading, I have no wish to bring you back from nowhere.

If however, you are prepared to deal with the profound mystery of name, form and Unity then you are in a position to love and be loved. You can dance with me. You can whisper in my ear all your dirty little secrets and I will love you still. This love is at once beyond any possibility of personality and intensely personal.

Our love exists not only in the archive of your experience but in the eternity of the Timeless. That I have never met you or touched your flesh in no way limits the completeness of my love for you. I speak, of course, of nothing less than the Love of Total Acceptance. To experience such love is to bathe in the radiant warmth of the fact you are perfect as you are.

May it find you now!

With Love,

Wayne

Hello my loves,

I love sex! I love the wildness of it. The way it rocks people out of their ruts. I delight in the continuing evidence that our control over it is tenuous at best. The ongoing sagas of powerful politicians, corporate and spiritual leaders brought down by lust played out in scenarios that can only be described as ludicrous, are mesmerizing. Each is a perfect opportunity to witness Powerlessness, though admittedly one that very few people seem to be able to take advantage of.

Part of what makes it all so dramatic is that public attitudes towards sex diverge so dramatically from what people actually think and do sexually. There are so many "shoulds" surrounding sex.

We are told:

"If you love someone you should not be interested in someone else sexually."

"Sex should be bound up with love. Sex "just" for fun is wrong."

"You should focus your sexual energy not on sex but on attaining spiritual Enlightenment."

"Sex is base and unworthy of a God oriented person," or on the other side, "Tantric sexual practice (with its emphasis on control) is the highest form of sex."

"You shouldn't have sex for money."

"You shouldn't have sex with someone of the same gender as you."

"Sex should be kind, gentle and caring."

"You should honor your sexual partner."

The list is nearly endless.

The problem, of course, is that it flies in the face of how human beings actually ARE!

The Living Teaching points to the fact that sex is an integral aspect of Life and Life is wild and dangerous, unpredictable and uncertain. Such reality stands in stark contrast to the FSA's compulsive claim of control. In fact one of the great spiritual fantasies is that when enlightenment is attained it brings with it perfect control. The fantasy posits that the sage controls his sexuality to the extent that, if it still continues to exist at all, its expression matches the prevailing moral code.

Life throbs, pants and pulses. It is a screaming orgasm that is equal parts pain and pleasure. In the simple Acceptance of What Is, sex (however it manifests) is met with Peace.

May it find you now!

Much love,

Wayne

Hello my loves,

   If I call you a spiritual seeker, are you offended? If so, no point in reading further, you are unlikely to benefit from any of the simple stuff I have to offer.

   If you ARE a spiritual seeker then chances are very good that you have read numerous spiritual books by numerous spiritual teachers. You have probably attended Talks, satsangs, retreats, conferences and meetings of various kinds. If you have a computer you will have undoubtedly surfed to websites, YouTube videos and webcasts. The result of all this is a dizzying cacophony of conflicting claims, concepts and ideologies. There are literally thousands of teachers, some living, others long dead. One tells you it is all a dream, another assures you it is the only reality. One says you don't exist, another says you absolutely do. One tells you you can do nothing, another insists you create everything and yet another slides in between to confidently explain you can only do one thing...wake up. Some take spiritual sounding names while others keep the names they were born with. Some dress in flowing, spiritual garb and others dress like ordinary people. Some are charismatic and charming, others are surly and unexceptional. Some insist that you must use your heart while others exhort you to use your mind. Some come from long established lineages, others assert that Enlightenment is a con. Nearly all warn about the dangers of the others.

   Of course, as a spiritual seeker, you have already seen all this. You don't need me to tell you it is a jungle out there. You have likely wrestled with the alligator questions of who is telling the truth and who isn't? Who is a genuine teacher and who is a poser? In the hope that you may derive the same benefit I received, I offer you the words of my guru, Ramesh S. Balsekar. He said, "the false guru and the genuine guru arise from the same Source." For me it was a potent pointer to the underlying perfection of it All.

May it find you now!

With much love,

Wayne

Hello my loves,

The love of the Guru is the greatest of gifts. It is without any conditions. You have done nothing to earn it and you need do nothing to keep it. It is without demands. It does not even require that you love the Guru back! You have this love despite your many shortcomings and defects of character. It is a love that meets you where you are and it accompanies you as you change. The love of the Guru is the Love of total acceptance. It includes everything and everyone...sinners and saints, beautiful and ugly, base and sublime alike. It is there even when you can't see it or feel it. It will not leave you for as long as you draw breath, because it is your birthright, your reward for being alive.

With Grace comes the knowledge of this unceasing love. May it find you now!

With love,

Wayne

Hello my loves,

It is only a couple of days since Guru Purnima (the full moon in July on which the Guru is honored and celebrated) and I have been basking in the glow of love, kindness and generosity that accompanied it. I relive the unequaled joy of my relationship with Ramesh when I see the pleasure of such devotion in the eyes of those who come to see me and in the words of those who write to me.

In the West to have a relationship as a disciple to a guru is often seen as an affront to independence and personal dignity. It is imagined that to have a guru is to surrender your personal power and in the West, particularly, personal power is itself the holy grail. The more personal power the better! It is not something to be given away. (The exception to this is in the clever strategy of giving up one's presumed personal power in order to amass far more potent spiritual power.)

To many in the West being a "disciple" is synonymous with being a "sucker." There are countless documented cases of gurus taking disciples money, having sex with their wives, daughters, pets and domestic livestock and just generally messing up their disciple's lives. I don't doubt that most of such accounts are substantially accurate. Both the East and the West are knee deep in horrible, inept and corrupt gurus. But like a lotus rising majestically from polluted muck the Guru appears as the light that pushes back the darkness.

The Guru is more than real. The Guru is reality itself. The Guru is omnipresent and eternal. The Guru dispels the illusion of personal power and reveals the Peace.

May it find you now!

With much love,

Wayne

Hello my loves,

The Bondage of Technique

Technique is the chain and the shackle.
It holds you and restricts you.
So softly padded
You hardly know it is there.

You like it because it is familiar
And carries the promise of control.
You imagine you can wield technique like a sword.
To protect and to conquer.

You are lured into the hamster wheel of progress
Momentarily exalted in the satisfaction of success.

But technique is a seductress
Promising more than she can deliver.

These promises entertain and distract you.
And while you dream of the glories of the Mastery to come
The stinging beauty of daily life passes unnoticed.

The Mastery of the sage is not of technique
The sage's Mastery is in his abidance in the ordinary!

May it find you now....

Much love,

Wayne

Hello my loves,

To awaken is to glimpse the Unity of all things. It is the beginning of the journey since only rarely does such insight endure. But once this awakening has happened it is impossible to return to ignorance. You are transformed. All who pursue the Living Teaching have already awakened to an expanded awareness. It is this that makes the experience of the Teaching possible. Life continues to unfold. The Teaching is ever present. The wave moves as the rhythm of the Ocean. Where you go, what you feel and what you do is clearly not in your hands.

Relax into this if you can. The more profoundly open to possibility you become, the more freedom you experience.

With Grace this freedom becomes the only Reality.

May it find you now!

With love,

Wayne

Hello my loves,

Have you ever had a visitor come from out of town and when you show them around you begin to re-appreciate the familiar things you have taken for granted? As your guest marvels at the plants and trees that to her are new and exotic, you start to REALLY see them again. The same is true for the quality of light in the sky and the traffic patterns and the architecture and the way strangers relate to each other as they pass on the sidewalk. You reawaken to the bird songs and the graffiti and the fashions and the smells that long ago had faded into the everyday.

The guru is simply that, a visitor from out of town, whose presence and consciousness point you to see what is HERE. The guru doesn't add anything...there is no need for him to...it is all already here.

With Grace, when the guru comes, you are able to invite him in, your heart opens and he shows you the miracles that abound everywhere you look.

May He find you now!

With love,

Wayne

Hello my loves,

Gratitude is the best! It is the ultimate human condition. When gratitude grips you, you are transformed. The world becomes a bountiful place. You know yourself to be blessed beyond measure. Your complaints fade away. Colors brighten. You feel wrapped in a blissful cocoon of gentle satisfaction. You are full. Nothing needs to be added or taken away. The irritations in your surroundings become muted and you know peace.

Gratitude itself is a gift. We do not manufacture it or will it into being. It comes, as do all things, in accordance with what Ramesh Balsekar called the Cosmic Law.

In the presence of gratitude, fear cannot survive.

May it find you now!

With much love,
Wayne

Hello my loves,

If you are spiritually advanced you know that the past, present and future all exist in Now. Still, in our humanness we perceive time progressively and consecutively. This is a good thing. Without the perception of the linear, everything would appear to happen at once and we would be infinitely busier than we already are!

One of the qualities of the lineality of time we don't like so much is the sense that we are bound by what came before. We often yearn to break free from the past. We want to reinvent ourselves, move somewhere else, take new names, change professions and mates. It doesn't work, of course. Never has. Who we are as people is infinitely more complex than a few, readily changeable aspects. We are actually the sum total of all that we have felt, thought and done before.

If we believe we are responsible for creating our lives then this enormous collection of past experiences is a huge burden to be dragged forward. In fact the sheer weight of the past is what inspires the idea that we should cut ourselves off from it and start fresh.

There is a different possible approach. It is to realize that in our humanity we are the creations not the Creator. To accept that we are as we are, the complex summation of all that has come before. And most importantly we must realize that change is inevitable and unpredictable. We are shaped by the past but we are not bound by it. Whether evolutionary or revolutionary, change happens. The butterfly was not bound by being a caterpillar. Its past was an integral part of what it is now.

Paradoxically, when this is fully seen, we realize we, as creations, are nothing less than the Creator made manifest.

May it find you now!

With much love,

Wayne

www.advaita.org

Made in the USA
Middletown, DE
13 May 2015